ETERNAL CARNIVAL

PAUL ZEPPELIN

ETERNAL CARNIVAL

iUniverse books may be ordered through booksellers or by contacting:

iUniverse
1663 Liberty Drive
Bloomington, IN 47403
www.iuniverse.com
844-349-9409

ISBN: 978-1-6632-2082-0 (sc)
ISBN: 978-1-6632-2085-1 (e)

Library of Congress Control Number: 2021906666

Print information available on the last page.

iUniverse rev. date: 04/05/2021

Foreword

Paul Zeppelin's masterfully written, vivid imagery passionately invites the reader to walk beyond the boundaries of their daily thoughts and emotions and helps them discover the layers of hidden happiness and suffering, of love and hate, of compassion and indifference. Paul's poetry is a multifaceted precious stone sharply reflecting his philosophy of hope and conveys his views and doubts, which are often controversial, yet always substantive through every verse. It triggers an intellectual or emotional response that may linger forever.

Epilogue

Reality only reveals itself when it is
illuminated by a ray of poetry.
Georges Braque

Contents

A Circus Left My Town

A circus left my town,
You heard the cheers,
I stayed. I am the clown
Who wipes your tears.

Look into my eyes,
Into these saddest wells.
Can't see the skies
Or even a home to dwell?

A circus left my town,
New dreams come true,
I am still a gloomy clown
Who laughs into the blue.

I've sinned, I fought,
I didn't love my foes,
Even in youth, I sought
A path from joys to woes.

Excitement left my daily maze,
I morphed into a self-effacing jester,
I am performing misery these days,
A sad burlesque is my ancestor.

A basement cannot be a gable,
I can't become a fiddler on the roof,
I played the Jack but never ran the table,
I laughed through tears in every spoof.

A bird may sing a song
And dive into the night,
Only a clown can't be wrong
Enjoying silence of moonlight.

A circus left my town,
I stayed, I am a clown.

A Crystal Shrine

I listened to your farewell song
Plunging into me out of nowhere,
The words were deathly wrong,
Your heart was never there.

I liked the language of your book
As sharp as your sarcastic mind,
You used an ax in every nook,
For our lies were tightly intertwined.

The ice masked our tiny creek
As if that wintry crystal shrine
Protected our family's mystique
From gloom of unavoidable decline.

Your thoughts in every phrase
Remind me of a freezing lace
Or rather of the dried bouquets
Forgotten in our marriage maze.

I hate small talk,
I tossed the dice;
But couldn't walk
Into that river twice.

War's over: collect your spoils,
Let's walk our isolated ways.
Just watch a pot that never boils,
Don't ever dream about faster days.

A Jester

I'm a mocking jester at the parties,
I entertain well-dressed pretenders
Appearing smarter than the smarties.
I wastefully tip half-baked bartenders
And swirl my wine in Riedel glasses,
Then toss my maxims to the masses:
"Don't shake your dandruff
On my shoulders,
Don't ever peddle my canoe,
Don't push into my stream
Your boulders,
Don't dump your melting ice
In my brew."

My wicked trickery still lingers,
It takes a snap of magic fingers
To throw an outrageous hissy fit,
It takes a witticism to leave a scar,
It takes a warbling of a nightingale
To turn this night into a day sunlit,
A tiny spark into a shiny superstar,
To turn a bass into a mighty whale.

To please my freakish muse,
I stand on shoulders of conformity,
Then rake my fruitless views
And join a nationwide absurdity
As a surreal jester at the parties,
As a strict juror of the smarties.

Reality dies out in disgrace,
Absurdity assumes its place.

A Spark of Hope

I am your shadow,
You walk, I follow you,
Don't say so long,
I am a bird, a swallow,
I am a song
That is forever new.

I pushed away my muse,
The one I fondly cherished;
I hardly have any excuse,
My newest verses perished.

I write a marathon of time
And never-ending plots,
I am an arrhythmic chime,
I disconnect the futile dots.

The Lady Justice isn't blind,
She is the heaven's dawn,
She is a harbor of my mind,
She is the greatest paragon.

I am St. Michael with a sword,
Kind to a foe and to a friend;
I am a guardian of our world
Unswerving to the bitter end.

Under the strands of rain
I am a spark of hope that's born;
I may not lose yet rarely gain;
Rejoice; it's not a time to mourn.

Feelings Deadened

I like the masquerades
Of the ancient Chinese,
So brusque and colorful,
But ready for the dates
With someone doubtful
Under the naked trees.

My feelings deadened,
My hopes have landed.
It was a hasty speech,
"Your eyes won't see me,
Your arms won't hold me,
You won't enjoy my love,
We won't be hand in glove."
I was offended:
"I am tired of your worries,
Please, stop, don't talk,
Don't ever preach;
I will drift alone
And find better glories"

I was a little muffled,
And simply ducked;
My feathers ruffled,
But not yet plucked.

Some fall into the sky,
Some soar to earth,
Some want to kill or die,
Some dream about birth,
Some live and learn,
Some love and burn.

Hare and Hounds

Don't try to stop a roaring train,
A symbol of unveiled aggression,
Our love will definitely die in vain,
Burned with the fire of our passion.

Where are the fallen on the battlefield?
I search as if I am a necromancer;
The sacred envelope is sealed,
No one has seen the answer.

Red cardinals would never fly
When yet another raven rules;
No one would even dare to try
To touch the egos of the bulls.

Life is a game of hare and hounds.
Life is the maze we always blame
For making our pointless rounds,
For lack of money or even fame.

I Am a Scholar

I visit graveyards as a tourist,
I see the stars, I see the crosses,
I am a scholar, not a jurist,
I count draws, victories, and losses.

I eat with cattle from the trough,
While I am sipping Guinness beer;
I never take my raincoat off,
I am not welcomed here.

I can no longer wait,
I am living as a hostage,
A prisoner of love and hate;
The chains don't let me write
About premonitions in the past,
About yesterdays of my tomorrows.
The angels didn't see me; they passed,
And I am left alone with my nasty sorrows.

Life squeaks with rusty hinges;
Days, weeks and even inches
Will not explain my deep dispair;
I have arrived to understanding
Of filigree in dusty unsophisticated dives;
Besides, in the beginning or the ending
Of everlasting brutal and waisted lives;
No one is ever gracious neither fair.

And yet, my glass is filled with grief,
Even a miserable life is awfully brief.

I Am a Tenacious Doctrinaire

I am melancholically insane,
My thoughts don't need a mike,
They are as loud as a hurricane,
You may adapt them if you like.
I am not a part of history,
I am just a living sequel,
I cracked the morbid mystery,
I am a cannon fodder a la carte,
Forever separate but equal.

We're collecting shattered bits
Of our horrible self-hating wits,
We imitate insanity of our gods,
And value their approving nods.
No wonder, we invented bliss,
And left the fiery deep abyss
Without any loyalty to friends,
To wives, and wedding bands.

Living alone creates a precious plus,
I am learning more about me and us;
I am a tenacious doctrinaire,
I entertain some of my principals
By playing a game of Solitaire
Without chatty and annoying pals.

Memory loss unlocked the door
Into nirvana, into the state of grace:
There is no boss, no peace, no war,
Only a mirror with my smiling face.

I Am Alone Against the Sea

The starry sky already fell,
A flock of seagulls screams,
Am I in Heaven or in Hell?
Am I encircled by my dreams?

I am alone against the sea,
Like Hemingway's old man,
As tides of a sadistic glee
Rotate my dinghy like a fan.

A naughty dawn
Sends me a breeze,
The moon is gone
I almost rest in peace.

A rapture for a jolly mind,
I scream at dead-beat boat,
It seems the sails resigned,
The stubborn stars still float.

I am still a mighty oak,
My branches push the sky,
But I am old, I cannot walk,
And cannot say goodbye.

I fan the flames
Of my illustrious days
Into lackluster nights
To cheer some names
That climb a staircase
Toward eternal lights.

It is a time to stop and rest,
To take my lifelong inventory,
I try to do my very best,
I only try to tell my story.

I Am Given by the Zodiac Two Fish

Beer foam is like a sparkling dew,
I blew it off into a craving grass,
I must admit, I swigged a few,
And guzzling yet another glass.

I am insane,
I try to catch descending stars,
But only make a heartfelt wish
To quit my drinking in the bars.
I fear, it is in vain,
The zodiac awarded me two fish.

Raindrops burst in a puddle,
The sun hides out in an overcast,
My spoiled saint decides to cuddle,
Although, this soppiness won't last.

I watched a movie from a dying past,
A sentimental image sprung to mind
From shattered porcelains of pain;
It was a captivating precious find
Out of classic movie telecast,
Gene Kelly's dancing in the rain.

My melancholic drinking did me in,
I croaked, I died, I took it on the chin.

My soul reversed a latch
And pushed the door.
There stood a batch
Of sinners hymn-singing

At my tomb,
I wonder how many siblings
Came from my poor mother's womb.

Raindrops burst in a muddy puddle,
Even my saint has no desire to cuddle.

I Envied Edgar Allan Poe

I met the ominous, cruel raven
That visited with Edgar Poe;
The bird veered near my haven,
I heard his croaking at the door:
"Forget your gentle muse Lenore,
You'll never see her anymore."

I stood in reservations to my knees
As if I didn't write my "Naked Trees",
As if I didn't write it apropos;
I truly envied Edgar Allan Poe;
I am still poor; he rolled in dough

I guess I am an old black raven,
I am not a gracious, striking swan,
I have committed all those seven,
Even my better days have gone.

Straight from the horse's mouth:
I took my quiet parting shower;
My hopes and I will die tonight;
I am a little acrimonious and sour;
And yet before I bought the farm,
I went to bed, turned off the light,
And stretched to set a fire alarm.

I Left My Footprints

That morning was tongue-tied,
Only a tormented evening cried:
A poet, their beloved boy
Was killed in a satanic ploy.
The skies turned gray
Above advancing flames
Lengthwise the perpetual runway
For worthy yet unknown names.

My life is like those boring books
Without epitaphs and epilogues
But with the well-illustrated pages
For each of the seven mortal sins;
A dire conception of our hypocrisy,
With the awe-inspiring shiny yoke
Of iron chains and golden cages.

Only the birds sing free,
They live in bliss; they live in glee.
They sing for all the helpless,
And for the mighty of this world;
They also sing for me.

I burned my cherished strophes,
My critics won't get any trophies:
I left my footprints on the path
Connecting life and death.

I am told, my verse, at times,
May take one's breath away;
I truly hope my modest rhymes
Will climb up heaven's stairway.

I Look Over the Fence

I dream about France,
About Italy, about Spain,
I look over the fence,
And buy a ticket for a plane.

I look for the greener grass,
And dream of a higher goal,
My life is like a broken glass,
Lying shattered on the floor.

I learned much more
Than meets the eye:
I was born to crawl,
But learned to fly.

I Play

The raindrops fall,
I pull my barge
Upstream,
Life is a constant brawl,
The world is justly large,
For my vast self-esteem.

I entertain a famous line:
"Until a bottle is uncorked,
Its pedigree is just a fable",
My steak is gently forked,
My friends enjoy the table.

I play a brainy game
What's in the name?
Responds were lame
Pride, vanity or fame.

If skin is in the game,
My hopes and senses
Stay quiet at the table;
I guard my name,
I take my chances,
At times, I raise a saber.

I genially appreciated
This fanciful retreat,
Albeit I really waited
To get my perquisite.

I Write

There is an epidemic of depression
Among the selfish, spineless youth;
They didn't inherit our aggression,
They never knew our past and truth.
They seldom use the rearview mirrors,
They are not fond of the fallen heroes.

I push a very weighty cart
Full of my verses and their criticism;
It rolls like a hollow broken heart,
Like a safe haven for my egoism.

Could it be a breath of fresh air
Or my poetic bar moved lower?
Or maybe as a compulsive voyeur
I saw the truths no one could bear?

I am surrounded by haunting images
Bonded with tiny niceties of my craft
That seek access to my sub conscience;
They quickly channel grim results
Into the sensuous minds and hearts
Of gullible and glee-intoxicated readers;
Then even a reluctant player
Participates in this seductive game.

Love at first sight?
What is there left for me to do?
I write...

My Quiet Morning Walk

It was a symphony of passion,
It was a vivid masterpiece of love,
It was another psychiatric session,
It was the most phantasmagoric bluff.
But then a psychedelic requiem arrived,
The bottom line of lives uneven or deprived.

I dwell on something metaphysical
Instead of something pure and lyrical;
At times, reality is like a falling knife,
Our life is not a dreary wife
We fall, we hit the bottom but can't divorce;
It is a genuine confession, not a true remorse.

I live as if my money blooms and grows
On a mighty maple tree;
I take my time to watch two croaking crows
Trailing behind a red-tailed hawk,
That flies into the endless glee
Above my quiet morning walk.

It's my legitimate birthright
To dump the fool
And choose the bright
To play the eight-ball pool
Or a sophisticated chess.
I know, I don't have to guess.

I left my conscience at the door,
I touched the gates of bliss,
It's not the end of our bloody war,
I only sway on our history's trapeze.

My Verses Flow

I was on pins and needles
Since I arrived into this world;
The yield was rather seedless,
I failed; my mother cut the cord.

My expectations are not justified,
I am serving poems on the side.

My timid inspiration froze,
I lived a life of hollowness
With its enormous power,
I wrote my terrifying prose
In a neglected dusty nest,
Where even Gertrude's flower
Looks like a daisy, not a rose.

I could no longer hope and wait,
I have only a little time to write,
I may become a gentle saint
When I am ready for the flight.

I am digesting what I feel and see,
I am trying not to bite the hooks,
I navigate the endless human sea,
And send typhoons into my books.

I left the swamp of emptiness,
I didn't grab the final straw;
I flew into a loneliness
To navigate my verses' flow.

My Will is Signed

My relatives are drunk,
They bashfully lie
From the dark corners
Of my room;
My future sunk,
Only the sober mourners
Frankly cry;
The clouds tensely sway,
The shadows sadly loom,
And veil the Milky Way;
They've read my will,
My last completed task,
They peeled away
My happy mask.

Leave me alone, unchain.
I lost my tortured mind,
I am happily insane,
My final will is signed,
Just pay the toll,
Don't soothe my soul,
I cannot fall,
I crawl…

Only the Fools Predict Tomorrows

Only the fools predict tomorrows,
Even the snipers miss their aims:
The wise men crawl into their burrows,
And making up the newest TV games.

Our history would never teach us anything,
But punishes for not remembering its lesson;
We didn't care to learn about David's sling,
But learned to pull our Smith and Wesson.

We think the horse of history needs spurs,
We want to leap into the future right away;
We kindly let our poets write another verse,
And serve it to the normal people on a tray.

I was too drunk, I acted like a pet,
When all the others got their loot;
I overslept and didn't place my bet,
The history will say, I shot my own foot.

The essence of integrity in our history
Is our given word; a promise kept;
I learned the axioms of history too late,
No explanation, excuse; I simply wept,
And promised, not to miss the final date.

Requiem

I studied mysteries of helium,
I learned to catch a falling knife,
I only couldn't face the tedium
Of introducing death to life;
I simply lived a few more years,
And lured a few more volunteers.

I didn't stack my deck,
I ran from heat to chill,
I was a nervous wreck,
But still enjoyed the thrill.

No one can have two deaths,
But one, no one can ever miss,
There are no avenues or paths,
But just a single stairway to bliss.

Rains shower my footprints,
The music bleaches them,
Today, my intellect commits
To visit ancient Bethlehem.
I crave to see the Holy place;
My thoughtful about-face.

My intellect is freed,
My eyes refuse to cry,
My heart refuse to bleed,
My soul has learned to fly.

I am a nemesis of death,
I trust, the requiem of Mozart,
Awaken by my farewell breath
Will resurrect my lifeless heart.

Rewards are on the Way

A silence yesterday,
A suicide tomorrow;
God sowed the waste,
We reaped the sorrow.
Dishonesty was placed,
By Adam and by Eve;
Rewards are on the way
While we still grieve.

I drenched my life
In wine and scotch;
It was a horrid botch,
I lost my gorgeous wife.

The gold of our years,
The silver of my hairs,
The sapphire of your eyes,
The crystals of your tears,
The swamp of my affairs,
The nonsense of my lies,
The honey of your pardon;
It started in the Eden's garden.

I lived in a free-thinking world,
Where no one fell from grace;
I wrote a verse or two
To mention to my Lord
When I will touch his face
Unblemished as morning dew.

Rothko

Beneath the multilayered harmony and dreams
Of Mark Rothko's perpetually enchanting art,
The foggy world of self-indulging warmly gleams,
But entertains my eyes; never my heart.

His paintings overwhelm,
They grasp my eyes;
Mark Rothko stirs the helm,
My freedom is my price.

Ebullient and energetic,
Phlegmatic and kinetic,
Perpetually depressed;
A victim of his brutal quest.
Both, intimate and grandiose,
Both, gentle and intimidating
His art was a true lethal dose...
Eternal heaven is still waiting.

Mark led me to the end of land
Where the sea of whims begins,
I leave behind my seven sins,
And learn the truth firsthand.

Solace

I am hammering on a Steinway
Proudly looming on its legs,
Three swollen shiny pegs,
Three judges of my play.

Nobody reads Euripides or Sophocles,
Nobody knows Antigone and Medea;
Only a merciless sword of Damocles
Decapitates a treacherous idea,
And saves our annoying world,
Or starts anew with a well-known word.

I dance away from ancient questions
To my rather evasive convoluted brain,
Which knows all the answers
But never straight as rain.

I effortlessly find solace in knowing
That repetition is a form of change;
The last and final bastion of hopes,
Lit by the ambers friendly glowing,
Reminds me of a life as a firing range,
Or happy nooses at the end of ropes.

I just renamed my old address
From Golgotha to Calvary
Without any problems or a stress:
No changes in our historic gallery.

Sufficient and Necessary

Some say my deeds are not
Sufficient and necessary;
I fry potatoes in an old teapot,
I drag my fishnet to the prairie.

Aroused curiosity will kill a cat,
It leads a wise man to the trap,
I promise to devour my old hat
If we and animals won't overlap.
We'll meet at the gates of hell
Whether we used to sour or fell.

Forget these deadly games
Of pass the buck
And kick the can;
No goals, no aims,
No fool's or Irish luck;
I only bring about what I can,
Then turn all things around,
And try to win my final round.

The end of life; my wobbly feet
No longer stomp the grass,
They only slide and gently treat
The autumn's tarnished brass.

I am not coming back;
The winter of my life
Stubbornly follows on my track,
Anticipating a triumphant strife.

The ends will never meet,
A life is a one-way street....

That's All She Wrote

Don't offer me your heart,
I am not that wise and smart
To shelter such a costly gift;
Without a heart we only drift.

The sun makes rainbows,
Above the flower beds;
A cupid shoots his arrows,
We turn into the newlyweds.

Loves are the ways,
Never the happy ends,
Loves are the preys
Of our wedding bands.

If we believe in love,
A miracle occurs;
It is a fountain of glee
Under a quilt of melancholy;
At times, it is enough,
It is what love prefers
Instead of a stairway to glory.

A sign on each tombstone
Presents the happy end,
That's all she wrote
To her best friend.

The Apples of Cezanne

I bit an apple painted by Cezanne
And broke my tooth,
I painted apples like Cezanne
And saw the truth.

It helped me to unlock the doors
Into the world of real arts,
Into the enigmatic chores
Of yet cold-blooded hearts.

A quick symbolic intertwining
Of darker days and lighter nights,
Ceased fights of life and art;
I turned the lights, I played my part,
And stopped the whining;
Then chose the labyrinths of science
But didn't invite a nasty dissonance
Into my measured life;
Her lacy lovely dress was white,
It was a wedding dress,
She has become my wife...

The space obtained the forms,
Some birds, some worms;
A preacher couldn't preach,
A teacher wouldn't teach...
We rediscovered our berth,
And peace descended on the Earth.

I've seen the other side of paradise,
It was absurd, horrific and obscene.
I've seen the other side of hell

It was quite friendly,
It was doing well
In these compelling exhibitions.

I hold my steaming coffee cup,
My lovely wife still wants to talk
The winds are waking up
To entertain my morning walk.
.

The Artist of My Last Sunset

I wandered in the fertile field,
The scaffolds were already built,
I am the artist of my last sunset,
I'll paint the sky in a bloody red.

The scars of country roads
Cross paths and rivers grid,
The rude dim-witted hordes
Worship their gods of greed.

I watch that tragedy parade,
I watch that puzzling charade,
Being just at an arm's length;
Integrity, I'll be your guard,
Humanity, I'll be your bard
Till truth is in my strength…

The verses run into my book
Like rivers rush into the sea,
I am utterly forever hooked,
I am chiseling my final plea.

It is my final throw of the dice:
I drape my words in Esperanto,
I struggle like a cow on the ice,
My verse is underdone al dente.

And yet, most gifted people
Appreciate the nature's call,
They tightly hold the bridle,
Their Pegasus won't ever fall.

The Book Is Wrong

My goals are frozen,
It is a soaring vanity
Of business meetings;
My path is chosen,
It is the night's insanity
Of gambling whippings.

I saw a slot; put a few quarters
Then held the reins in hand,
My verses slipped into the land
Of merciless gambling slaughters.

Casino is a miserable bride,
The Queen of broken hearts;
I grit my teeth and ride
Against the decks of cards,
And only my illusions
Will never rest in peace
In quagmires of confusions
Imagining a morning breeze.

The Book is wrong,
Those who don't work
Will always get their feed,
And won't erase their smirk.
Because they hear
In every psalm and song,
What is to them so dear:
Eternity of vanity and greed.

The Books of Knowledge

The books of knowledge
Have no written pages.
An early dawn lifted the yoke
Of our nightly heavy blankets;
The beams of ever gentle sun
Caress my wallpapered walls;
I watch the troubled world
Through crooked windows.

I see the flirting pirouettes,
The day is young and shy,
Two dancing silhouettes
Descending from the sky.
I gulped a precious spark
Of my awakened thought,
As if am a rare unhappy lark,
As if am an uninvited ghost.
I put my best foot forward,
Ready for dancing in the rain,
The boss of our selfish world
Arranged a spiteful hurricane.

The sideline of the world,
The cowards' paradise:
I scream but cannot close
My numb wide-open mouth,
Then cover my eyes to see
The frozen image framed.
I hear the loud symphony
Of my unbearable alarm.

Don't wake me up,
Don't steal my dream,
Just pass my cup of tea,
Allow me to watch my film,
The books of knowledge
Have no written pages.
The cinema of daily life
Changes its seasons;
The Holy Virgin pledges
Concord to our battlefields;
While we write our hollow
Books of reasons.

The lighthearted blossoms,
The fragrant gifts of springs,
The existential classrooms
Teach us to fly without wings.

The Braves Without Fear

The rains of yesteryears
Won't satisfy gods' thirst,
The braves without fears
Are fated to die first.

Tall mountains protect my secrets,
Fast running rivers wash my sins,
I waste my days in sequence,
Count the losses, ignore the wins.

I am in crosshairs of duality,
One hair pulls me from left to right,
The other pulls me up and down;
One day, I am unquestionably bright,
The other, I am a pointless silly clown.
I try to justify finality of a bullseye,
Blaming mortality of every passersby.

I pull the strings of my marionettes,
The others win, I only place the bets.
My healthy pride was stolen
And silence filled the void,
Even my ego, usually swollen
Was mercilessly destroyed.
I am mean mugging for a photo
Or laughing ear to ear,
I am diverting violence and slaughter
For those who try to kill a puppeteer.

I am collecting info from the table
Of those who dig foxholes and fight,
Of those who are talented and able,
Of those who bring the blinding light.

The night is over; new dawn is here,
I am a leafless clover; I lost my fear.

The rains of yesteryears
Won't satisfy my thirst,
The braves without fears
Are destined to die first.

The Brazen Horse of Life

Ecstatic as a little boy,
I walked along deep wells
Of endless joy
And heard the silver bells.
I fervently embraced
The faking gospel singers,
My youth has been erased,
Yet my nostalgia still lingers.

No one is infinitely obeyed
Or earned to guard the Gates,
Even the law obeying saints
Are unrecognizably decayed.

Even in despair, I get to ride
The brazen horse of life,
I want to see the bitter side
Of every useless strife
Between unsighted forces,
And only then, at night,
Can I pen my defiant verses.

The inevitability of death
Amazed my vulnerable youth,
I couldn't catch my breath.
Much later, I discovered truth:
There is no paradise,
Poor Judas landed on dry ice,
Eleven went to the abyss,
Only the Saver soared to bliss.

Embalmed by my retiring art,
Evil and good are intertwined
In every mind and heart
Of friends left far behind,
In every memory retouched
By its creator, yet unmatched.

The Burden of Deceit

The burden of deceit,
Of daylong pressures
May lead you to defeat
Of our lifelong treasures.

It is much easier to ask
For a mere forgiveness
Than for permission,
Just do your business;
Some have a task,
Some have a mission.

Why don't you take a chance
And bend the law sometimes?
You will get a priceless glance
At punishments and crimes.

Try to be an arsonist or a thief,
You dreamed of this from birth;
Your sentence will be brief,
And turn into a pleasant mirth.

The prison walls and iron bars
Protect you from a daily strife,
From worthless, vulgar farce
Of what we call a normal life.

The Burden

The pale and gloomy moon
Sobs over my lonely walk,
I truly hope to see you soon,
Right after I defeat my yoke.

The burden of my past,
The salty sea of tears
Is still too deep and vast;
After so many quiet years,
Our fields of fertile soils
Still heal the shame of spoils.

I silenced my dire past
And loved again, at last.

I drank the nectar of your kiss,
You melted in my arms tonight,
I stroked your hungry knees,
And disappeared inside...

Your scream still hovers
Above two shaky lovers.
Self-deprecating lingerie
Covers the pain of glee.

The Burial of Snow

My granny's lilac garden died,
Sad branches waved farewell,
The skies and clouds cried,
After the lifeless petals fell.

I left that walled and distant town
Of innocence and dreamy wishes
For life among the wicked powers,
Where everybody wears a crown,
Piles loots into the darkest niches
Behind the needle-woven flowers.

Self-shielding, chronic urges
Of my overwhelming sadness
Survived the merciless purges,
Survived the pointless madness
Of murderers and total strangers;
Yet when I lost my will to strive,
Only the damned and fallen angels
Calmly whispered, "Paul, stay alive"

Isaiah screamed,
"Spears into pruning-hooks,
Swords into ploughshares!"
Regrettably, he vainly dreamed,
Today, nobody reads smart books,
The history repeats, nobody cares.

The rite of spring
Running the streams of thaw,
And bringing nightingales to sing
Above the burial of winter's snow.

The Calendar of Fate

My woefully unfit creator
Forgot my birthday date,
A pie arrived much later
Into the calendar of fate.

Spring winds don't blow anymore,
There is no milky cloud in the sky,
There is no one to keep the score
Of those who'll never get that pie.

They throw themselves into a day,
At night, come home on feet of clay,
Exhausted horses of a steeplechase,
To get some rest before another race.

Lackluster schedules
Of a bourgeois routine
Led me into surrender
To dogmas of despair,
Into desire of splendor
I never learned to bear.

I am not yet driving on the asphalt,
I am still crawling through the ditch,
Only my fortune's somersault
May pull me out of this glitch.

Life was a shooting range
Connecting hell and bliss,
I will embrace the change,
No matter, hit or miss.

The happy bliss is overpopulated,
The empty hell is bored to death,
For eighty years I humbly waited
To send away my farewell breath.

The birthday pie arrived too late
With dripping candles of my fate.

The Chill of Sweat

The chill of sweat,
The heat of fear,
The lethal threat,
The end is near.

I hear the crowd cheers,
I see her wedding gown,
My fortune calmly veers,
I entertain before I drown
In my sentimental tears.

I clawed my wings,
I left my hopes behind,
The bell already rings,
My guilty plea is signed.

Earth has no corners,
Don't even try to hide,
Among the foreigners;
Trust me, enjoy the ride

I still don't know why,
So long, adieu, bye-bye.

The Crunchy Boneyard

What's life? No one yet knows;
Life soars from yesterdays,
And veers between tomorrows,
Yet seldom leaves a trace.

The crunchy boneyard
Of a weary summer
That turns into a fall,
Becomes a postcard
Of a gilt newcomer
Which learns to stroll.

Whether I hold or fold,
I am at the threshold
Of a splendid life,
Though most foretold
That I will win this strife.
Those wishes lasted
Until they faded;
I firmly trusted
That life is the purest gold.
Life was a little overrated.

Even in our metric age,
I am more than six feet tall,
I am not an actor on the stage,
Life is no longer a masked ball.

The Fruits of Art

The fruits of love
May die in time;
The fruits of art
Will live forever;
Therefore, a loving dove
Is smart yet never clever
Like a disregarded mime
With his cold-blooded heart.

As a young poet I was poor;
The older Brits would say,
I whistled through my fist:
Just thirst and hunger, no amour,
I was not loved, I was not kissed,
I ghostly marched on feet of clay.

I tried to put my verses
On the business rails,
I rode my horses,
I turned my sails,
But not a single penny
Fell into my wallet;
Whatever you may call it,
I truly didn't want too many.

Reality was not congruent
With my immaculate desires;
My dreams were ruined;
I didn't quit; I changed the tires.

The Lackeys

The TV pundits talk and urge,
The politicians beg but splurge,
Their speeches are red-hot,
They shake your hand,
They kiss your butt,
Yet are still able to grandstand

I'd rather be a loud moneychanger,
I'd rather be a cruel prison ranger,
I'd rather be a beacon to nowhere,
I'd rather be a nose-chained bear.

While licking asses of your bosses,
Wipe your brown lips and noses;
They let you lick but not to bite;
I hope you have a lovely sight.
The lackeys of the world, unite!!!

The Lamb

I read a song of William Blake,
The sadness of "The Lamb",
My tired mind attempts to rake
His poetry into a messy jam.

I am in pursuit of kindness,
I want to soothe his pain,
I need and long for guidance,
I soak in doubts of the rain.

I knew about Judas' mission,
And Peter's three disgraces,
The Pilate's painful decision
And Magdalene's embraces.

Through silence of the crowd
The Lamb returned to see us,
To see a symbol of my doubt,
The finger of apostle Thomas.

A blanket of dark clouds
Hides our futility at night,
And validates my doubts
For strangers in plain sight.

In hunt for a mere kindness
My chances are quite bleak;
I need your guidance,
Dear Lamb, I am weak.

The Last Supper of a Sinner

Hello, waiter, please, give me a table,
Pour wine of the best French label,
Remind the chef to pay attention,
I am here to spend my total pension.

Tonight, I drink and eat,
Tonight, I certainly enjoy it,
Tomorrow, I'll dazed and sigh,
Tomorrow, they'll turn the switch
And I'll die....

Thank you,
For the Last supper of a sinner;
My curfew
Was commanded till this morn;
I thought you knew,
My dinner was a real winner;
Goodbye, no one will mourn,
Adieu.

The Rainbow Arched

The rainbow arched
Above green shoots,
And reached its goal.
The ravens marched
In dirty heavy boots
Across my tired soul.

The strong-willed crows
Annoyed and chased away
A few young red-tailed hawks;
They simply tried to decompose
The vows of predators and prey
About amity among the flocks.

I hate the crows and ravens,
The messengers of nights,
The tenants of dark havens
And graveyards of the lights.

I watch my earnest foes,
And learn their flaws,
I like debates and talks,
I win or lose and yield;
I wonder why the hawks
Flew from the battlefield.

I squeeze my pointed line
Through a stone-cold pearl,
I carve my wicked rhyme,
And dream of hawks that swirl.

The Same Old Team

I scratch my seldom pretty lines
In smoky music filled hangouts,
Then pay my illegal parking fines,
And drive away with drunken doubts.

But later with a vicarious passion
Of a nonbeliever conning priest,
I say, God, let me be old-fashioned,
I am just flour waiting for some yeast.

Comparison is the quiet thief of joy,
A competition is the devil's ploy
That heartlessly divides
The ripples and the tides.

Before, I paid a weighty toll,
Last night, the fare was lighter;
I'd turn the other cheek or crawl;
Last night I dared to be a fighter.

In strife you are a predator or prey,
Don't tease yourself, don't dream,
No one can be above the fray,
We are playing for the same old team

The Satan's Ball

The dollar takes a walk,
The virtue never follows,
Some are forever broke,
Some cast no shadows.

The sinking ship of fools,
The blind pilots the blind
Across the dry well pools,
The reasons stay behind.

The Satan's masquerade,
The bonfire of the greed,
The mob came to parade,
The chewers of the feed.

The treasuries are down,
The yields are looking up,
The speculators drown,
I wouldn't help or interrupt.

Long live the greed,
The greenback rules,
Some laugh, some bleed,
The Shabbat of the fools.

Life of the greed,
The Satan's Ball,
Day of the Wall,
Day of the Street.

The Shadows Weave a Farewell Shroud

The shadows weave a farewell shroud,
The clouds weep above the battleground,
His image pales, he died, so I can breathe,
I brought to him and laid a modest wreath,
I lost another brother to the greedy war,
He never knew what he was fighting for.

The Silver Lining

I lovingly caressed the silver lining
Of tortured souls turned inside out,
The sins were never rinsed by rain,
And yet I never heard their whining
As if the hotness of a cruel drought
Eternally dispersed the tears of pain.

Our daily resurrected sun
Sends down sparkling stars,
They are descending one by one
We make a wish and heal our scars.

My life is pure as a newborn baby
And innocent as flowers of spring,
Sometimes, impatient as a lady
Unless she gets a wedding ring.

The Silver Rings of Smoke

The silver rings of smoke,
The handcuffs of my treasures,
The chains of promises I broke,
The wedding rings of pleasures.

The silver rings of smoke,
The haloes of my angels
That flaunt me as an oak
Among the frailer strangers.

The silver rings of smoke,
I dip the end of my cigar
In scotch and let it soak,
Then pinch my old guitar.

The silver rings of smoke,
You help to dump my yoke,
You help to write my verse
As Pegasus, my loyal horse.

The silver rings of smoke,
The crispy bagels in the air,
When chefs put on a toque
And sport their foreign flair.

The silver rings of smoke
Have risen to a better world,
I'll join them when I croak
After I write my final word.

The Skies are Sealed

The shepherd told my heart,
"Your soul is the finest art,
Your body is a cozy manger
For Lucifer, the fallen angel."

The skies are sealed,
The fluffy lazy clouds
Are basking in the sun;
I am rambling in the field,
Away from noisy crowds,
As if I am a banished nun.

In the beginning
We heard the primal word,
We even knew the meaning
Of our wisdom's risen sword.

The creed of Nicene,
Three hundred-twenty-five,
Was the first seething scene
Of our religious power strive.

All angels are asleep or busy
While we are crammed
Like bubbles in a beer;
We are afraid to take it easy,
I am sure, I will be dammed
For I unveiled our sticky fear.

I am a tracker of delights,
I shoot malaise of darkness,
I crave the sunny daily sights;

I learned amid my daily finds
The sun every so often blinds;
Only the darkness at its best
Brings us a mighty starkness
Of ceaseless peace and rest.

The Sky is Weirdly Dark

The sky is weirdly dark,
Under the hail of pearls;
A solitary vulture twirls
Above the rainbow arc.

I bowed my head,
Buttoned my jacket,
And plunged both hands
Into my empty pockets.

I like the requiems of storms,
The symphonies of death,
When angels blow their horns,
I barely catch my breath.

The end of the known world
In Sodom and Gomorrah,
The judgment's risen sword
Was forged in the old Torah.

I sip my "Maker's Mark",
I can no longer drive or park,
Connecting dusk and dawn,
I am a singing, dying swan.

The world is mad,
The world is gored,
The world is dead,
Long live the world.

The Snow Falls

The snow falls,
We slowly walk,
Time shyly rolls,
We hardly talk.

Time slips away
Between our fingers,
We stay above the fray
As if our love still lingers.

Our dystrophic brains,
Half-baked and sick,
Pull our nuptial chains
Through thin and thick.

My bad luck bends,
The darkness ends,
It is my timely turn:
I place a hefty bet,
And I will try to learn
How to end our duet.

My never-ending memories
Produce clean conscience,
Produce unwanted worries
And free but garish lunches.

The Sounds Swirled

The sounds swirled
Like falling leaves;
The flags unfurled
Beneath the eaves.
Fourth of July,
Again, I am in happy tears,
You always asked me why
For rather countless years.

Life is a factory of fakes,
Life is a camp of forgers,
The nights are cemeteries
For our lost sweepstakes,
The days are our canaries
That die if a danger surges.

In spider webs of prisons
My innocence was killed,
In spite of cruel treasons,
I lived. My angels willed.
At last, I reached the end,
The goal of my pursuit,
A gift only the gods could
Send,
The Tree of Knowledge
Shared its priceless fruit.

Fourth of July,
The happy fireworks
Loudly cracked the sky,
Even the tough men cry.
Now you know why.

The Stars Fall from the Sky

The stars fall from the sky,
Two candles dimly glow,
I think you meant goodbye,
Why did you say hello?

Life is a locked up prison cell,
We circle on the endless noose,
It feels like a spinning carousel,
We turn but can't get loose.

Please, hold your horse,
I can no longer love you. Why?
It's getting only worse.
We are two planets in the sky.

The sun will always rise,
Each planet has its orbit;
Two shattered lives,
It is damn sad and morbid.

Blue skies melt in your eyes,
And run into malachite of grass,
The waterfall of tears and sighs,
Reflects the autumn's brass.

Sharp scissors of your legs
Walk through my loving heart;
Life stinks like rotten eggs,
Our sandcastles fall apart.

It is the end of our affair,
I cannot feel that you are mine,
Gray lace runs through my hair,
I cannot write a decent line...

I hold the bottle of my love,
The wine is luscious, very old,
I swirl the sediment and bluff
As if the trail is yet not cold.

Life hurled us far apart;
The darkest day on earth;
A sailboat of my heart
Forever left its cozy berth.

The Stars Fall

The stars fall
Into the seas,
The heaven parts,
The teardrops roll,
The laughter flees
From broken hearts.

Without a fair dream
The mighty laughter
Will cry and scream
Forever after.

I saw the tree of love,
A single apple fell,
For me it was enough
To learn about hell.

I stumbled over
My own footprints,
I thought I was sober
After a drinking.blitz.
I drank a lot today
To see tomorrows,
To wash or lob away
My whining sorrows.

Life plays the same
A hawk-dove game;
I live, I know sin,
I take, I give,
I can forgive,
I can forget,
I hope to win,
I placed my bet.

The Station Left my Train

The station left my train;
White virgin snow
Attempts to soothe my pain,
Although my scars still glow.

I want to groan and howl,
I lost my fight, I threw a towel,
But I was trained to smile,
I walk my miserable extra mile.

Dawn wipes my tears,
Dusk chains my fears,
In premonition of a glee,
I am learning to be free.

Having a friend like you,
I need no enemies at all;
I walk on morning dew,
And have no plans to fall.

I was informed that you were eager
From the get-go to pull the trigger.
And yet my poetry turned prose
When you became a wasted rose.

My passion was a welcomed treat,
I used to be as brave as a fire eater,
Today, I am washed out, I am beat,
I take from Paul and give to Peter.

I exercise a thriving lunacy
Of quarreling with freaks;
I still ignore a foolish legacy
Of turning other cheeks.

The station left my train,
Only the memories remain,
I am a hostage of that train,
I vain, it tries to soothe my pain.

The Straw in the Breeze

The straw in the breeze,
The scent of crispy hay,
The trees performing a striptease,
The freezing autumn has its way.

I choose the fastest lane
Against the headwinds of my pain,
I choose the tailwinds of my joy
Instead of living as a mere decoy.

A blanket of my comfort
Shelters lackluster days,
My life's elusive contour
Emerges in a misty haze.

I choose a fountain of life,
I choose a victory in strife,
I choose the sunsets in a flight,
Instead of sleeping pills at night.

The autumn paints the woods,
Delivers its abundant yields,
The sun caresses lonely fields,
Above the ancient lace of roots.

The youngsters dreamed of love,
The autumn cried, I had enough,
The pines dropped perky prongs,
The birds were tired of their songs.

The sun brought a jolly day,
Indian summer passed away,
New winter lives without a sin,
A gentle spring deserves to win.

The Street of Truth

Enough of sugarcoating,
I'm a ship that's floating,
I'm in a hurry to see gods,
I'm sure they lead a crowd
Of those who have the odds,
Of those who dare to doubt.

It is a time of crying walls,
Witnessing a horrid blight
Of our wolf-whistled souls,
Misled into the other fight.

So many days were wasted
Parading off the beaten path,
So many meals were tasted
To satisfy my starving wrath,
My sinful distrust of mavens
Aiding not saints, but ravens.

Today, I turn the ending page,
Today, I'm revisiting my youth,
Today, I'm free from futile rage,
Today, I walk the street of truth,
Today, I wouldn't fly too high
To see the other fallen angel,
Unless I wave my last goodbye
To a small baby in that manger.

The Strings of Silver

Years march in dirty boots
Across the fields of dangers,
Then dump their grimy loots
In front of the puzzled angels.

I have been "gently chided",
I took it as a "ton of bricks",
They called it "being guided"
Toward the hastening tricks.

Blind sadness of the moon
Cast scary random shadows,
Dawn left the nightly womb
To light the darkest hollows.

An angel guides me to the gates,
Don't leave my shoulder, please;
The winds whip the fallen leaves,
As if they dance with our dates.

The strings of silver in my hair,
The scorching avenues of rage,
The weighty yoke I hardly bear
Until I write my final page.

The Sun Has Washed Its Feet

The lightning left the sky,
The thunder talks to stars,
The fields are almost dry
Along the tractor's scars.

The sun has washed its feet
In quiet waters of my lake,
It was my unexpected treat,
A lavish icing on the cake.

I changed my horses
In life's unclear midstream;
I burned my verses
To hear their scream
Under the nightly clouds,
Under the moon half-dead,
Above our humble shrouds,
And our daily wine and bread.

Life killed my innocence,
Time crashed my youth,
Its meek axiomatic truth,
But skid my common sense.

My dreams were earned:
I've seen a human shark
Caught in the mousetrap,
The deserts died in freeze,
The world's been burned,
The seas gulped Noah's ark,
A gory war delivered peace
Packed In a tasteless wrap.

.

The Sun Moved Up

The sun moved up
Into a morning play
With sleepless skies,
Leaving its yesterday
To a chest-dip snow;
I rub my weary eyes,
I drink my coffee cup,
A day begins to glow.

Push came to shove,
I didn't stop the flare,
I couldn't say enough,
I wouldn't even dare.

Life is a dialog among
The deaf,
Life is a performer for
The blind,
There's no audience,
No coach, no ref,
Even a common sense
Was left behind.

My fate was baked
Into a godsent cake
As incarnation
Of my fears,
As a prearranged ovation
For the Holy Grail of tears.

I am writing in my fable
About ceaseless youth,
About yet unknown truth;

I am not a Pavlov's dog,
I am a wolf, I am rogue,
I howl if I see the moon
That flies above a gable.

We soar together
But always fall alone,
And wonder whether
To laugh or moan

The Sun Won't Rise

Our intellectual quagmires
Are timid carnivals of slugs,
We run into the sizzling fires,
Like bulls toward the red rugs.

I am torn between two poles,
I've read the Dead Sea Scrolls,
I have to feed a hungry mouth
Of curiosity for what it's worth.
I am square-dancing in the North,
I am playing Mozart in the South.

The sun won't rise; I can't but do,
The sun will set; I can but don't.
My own success was just a clue,
I placed my bet, the others won't.

Under the signs of Zodiac,
Gods give, gods take it back,
No one controls their moods,
No one would lift their hoods.

I soared into the skies
To learn my fate,
I met some other guys
Devouring artistic glee,
It was too late,
I got a mound of debris.

Fear is the source
Of every failure,
I never dated whores,
I never met my savior.

I never dated anyone
Within the internet,
I took a chance; fears gone,
I heard her yes before we met.

The Sunset of Our Love

The dim sunset of our love is here,
The words are slowly leaving our lips,
I offered all and nothing was too dear,
I needed time. You smirked: "No tips".

I knelt in my remorse, I cried, I knew
It would be hell on earth without you,
I begged, don't leave, I'll hit the bottom,
Give me a chance, small as a tiny atom.

A single chance and I'll earn forgiveness,
A single night and I'll earn your love again,
We will enjoy each day life gives us
Our love will make us both insane.

The moon will lose its half,
The churches' bells will ring,
The mockingbirds will laugh,
The nightingales will sing.

I am strong enough to hug you,
I am warm enough to kiss you,
I learned my rights and wrongs,
I will caress you with my songs.

Give me a chance,
Destroy the fence,
Remove the spell;
I am on my knees;
Is it the last farewell?
Is it the goodbye kiss?

The Sword of Damocles

I am a singing bard
Of all the seven sins
Of our faulty world;
I search the graveyard
Where our hell begins
With just a single word.

A sharp Damoclean sword
Hangs over my weary head,
I pledge, don't cut the cord,
I think, I am almost dead.

The darkness mingles
Bright stars and crescents,
The snow blanket lingers
Over my birthday presents.

Today, I am eighty-eight,
Leftovers of gray hair
Were waiting till this date
To boost my lifelong flair.

I am a proud dying swan,
Here is my deathbed plea:
Allow me to die at dawn,
Rejoice, don't cry for me.

Before eternity of bliss
I want your farewell kiss;
Please, hold my hand,
Please, call the band,
Let's tango on my bed,
I'll sleep when I am dead.

The Tango Ends

Bandoneons play
Their lovely notes;
The tango floats,
We slowly sway.

There are no friends,
No laughs or sorrows,
Nobody lends,
Nobody borrows.
We are in a trance,
We dance…

No one would paint
The other side
Of decorations;
Our vanity and pride
In vain, forever wait
A statute of limitations.

The music stops,
Euphoria no more,
The night descends,
We leave the floor,
The curtain drops,
The tango ends.

The Taste of Memories

We ran across the field,
I held your tender hand,
We had a family to build,
Our castle from the sand.

The taste of memories
Still lingers in my heart,
She liked plain remedies,
I welcomed poetry and art.
She left, she walked away,
Our love had feet of clay.

The pains that never pass
Destroy our happy cradles:
Love is not gold, but brass,
It only beams in our fables.

The Tasty Tidbits

My teary-eyed diaries of war,
At times, my healthy nihilism,
And a tad sardonic metaphor
Defeat their artsy symbolism.

My strophes moved
From violent to quieting,
No issues left untouched,
Each has been proved,
And shined like lightening,
Before a rainbow arched.

My trophies from Vietnam,
A gunshot and few scars,
A medal in my soiled palm,
Drunk buddies in the bars

Nothing is new under the sun,
From time to time, a better gun.
The same long bloody wars,
The same revolving doors
For those who lick the boots
Of those who have the fruits.

Gods never know our limits,
They only raise esprit de corps
Of those who fight their war,
By giving them the tasty tidbits.
Give us a finger, we'll grab a hand,
Give us a hand, we'll grab an arm,
I see no end to our endless harm.

No one is vigorous forever,
No one is a lifetime clever,
I hope my spring has sprung
And you'll hear my songs
That were unsung.

The Tea is Sweeter at the End

I cherish that evasive thread
Of gentle graceful footprints,
She went beyond the dread,
She kissed and I became a prince.

I am leaving my domain,
I lit and puffed my cigarette,
It was a red-light for the train
Which hasn't left the station yet.

The train will chug into the dusk,
The stars will swim away,
My life will shed the husk,
I will enjoy another day.

I faced my fragile dream,
I touched her tender hand,
She turned into a shiny beam,
The premonition of a happy end.

Life's given once for us to play,
It is so hard to find a real friend,
My granny used to say,
"The tea is sweeter at the end."

The Tears of Rains

Is there a better world
Somewhere?
Is there a dusty road
Into nowhere?
That road never ends,
Just veers,
Wise Moses learned
In forty years.

I think about birches,
Such sinless virtues,
So innocently white,
Gullible brides of light.

I am still looking for that path
Lost in the labyrinths of wrath,
I miss the birches of my youth,
The fragile innocence of truth.

There is a dying hope in me,
I haven't heard its final plea,
My deep nostalgic pain
Evokes the tears of rain.

The Thaw

The dog days play the blues,
I am writing lyrics every night,
Nevertheless, I failed to fuse
My desperation with delight.

My loyal Pegasus that I adore,
Obeys the outdated frozen law,
He acts as a converted whore,
While I am waiting for the thaw.

At last, the rite of spring,
The chilly days take wing,
The jolly sun directs its rays
To bake some breezy days.

Under a melting icy throw,
I hear the melodies of streams
And sparkly diamonds of snow
Whisper farewell to winter dreams.

Frost threw a tantrum
Like a naughty child,
A white gowned phantom
Of nasty winter long exiled.

I am writing history of times,
A necessary quid pro quo
For punishments without crimes,
Wrongly delivered centuries ago.

The truth destroys the frozen law,
Long live a baby-spring and thaw!

The Tired Moon Begins to Yawn

The glossy stars enjoy the float,
The tired moon begins to yawn,
The ripples shyly rock my boat,
Caressing silence before dawn.

The rules of my perpetual strive
Are muddled and obscure,
I hate to close my eyes and dive
Into the ocean of the vowed cure.

I lived my verdant youth,
Played "hide-and-seek",
Tried to escape the noose,
And turned the other cheek.

Freed from the vanished loves,
I dumped my chains and cuffs;
I am the happiest man alive,
I never close my eyes. I drive.

The Tragic End of Farce

The tragic end of farce,
The end of a lifelong rope;
Only the river of my hope
Rocking the fallen stars.

Successes of my strife
Won't justify my whims,
Flowery fables of my life
Bubbling above the rims.

I guess, I tried too hard,
My futile patience faded,
I pulled the winning card,
I bet and quickly made it.

Today, I am entirely
Devoted
To heal my sun-kissed
Mind;
Euclidean postulates if
Quoted,
Help me to lead the deaf
And blind.

I circle the perimeter
Of a knowledge earned;
I am afraid to get inside,
New thoughts are bitter,
The youngsters learned
That our own truth was
Crucified.

The Train of Life Stops Once

I hate the tears of rain,
Its penetrating crystal lines,
The silent screams of pain
Above the roads of rhymes.

Do not complain about life
To a merciless hangman,
He is not a careful midwife,
He has for you another plan.

The last train station,
The terminal of death,
The deathbed of creation,
The cradle of my breath.

I hear a sad goodbye,
Farewell to our alliance,
The train of life rolls by
And stops, but only once.

The Tree of Knowledge

Before I went to college,
Life pledged a honeyed sin
Of carnal knowledge
And let my happiness begin.

I sadly wander across the paths of glory,
Star-studded skies rest on my shoulders,
The idle moon majestically appears afar,
Reflecting light that lulls my aspirations.
I find healing in futile paranoiac dreams,
I leap over a few exhilarating moments,
Each happy day leaves a long shadow,
Descending from a crescent to the pits.

Some pledges to be kept
Above the chimneys' tops;
Too many actors to be swept
Before the final curtain drops.

The scratchy sweaters of sheepish clouds
Amassed like cotton balls in a crystal jar,
Waiting in vain, to fly at night without aim.
A poet screams, "I see the strings of rain
Piercing my cliquey oneness with the land,
Flaunting its innocence completely naked."

I am a brick-and-mortar guy, one size fits all,
The sun can't honor my desires and wishes,
The end; I am a human hound in the pursuit
Of a reckless soul within my skinless being.
I am wearing poisoned ivy of my bitter years,
The flow of a hurried time erased my voice,
My wishes drowned in the river of my tears,
The angels blessed my self-effacing choice.

Regrettably, the stars were violently young,
Quietly becoming much gloomier in a flash.
A single song remained unsung,
The parting song of a dying swan.
Some embers didn't expire in ash,
Life brought a gentle light of dawn.

The Trees are Still in Leaf

I hit the bottom of the well,
Its goodness doesn't taint,
This mesmerizing marvel
Doesn't allow us to faint.

All started with the word,
I truly took it on the chin,
But didn't stop the world;
It will continually spin.

Our pursuit of happiness
Is a chaotic gloomy mess;
I am a want-to-find hound,
Chasing a merry-go-round.

I climbed the wall of worry
To see the Promised Land;
I couldn't write a better story,
I came without glee in hand.

The trees are still in leaf,
The autumn lost its friends,
They ran away in disbelief;
Means justified the ends.

The Trees Got Cold

Even the trees get cold,
They cough and sneeze;
We kill their hopes,
We burn their slopes;
They shed the autumn gold,
And tremble in the freeze.

The continents of our loaded past
Scarred with the seas and rivers,
We shred our memories to slivers,
And mix the takers with the givers.
Four tinted horsemen are too fast,
Only the mountains will outlast

It is not very easy to forget,
It is much harder to forgive;
Life is a never-ending debt,
Life is a sin no one can outlive,
Life is a nervous masochist
Who's longing for a madness;
Life is a miserable sadness
Of a devout, self-denying nun,
Who never had a hit-and-run,
Or even passionately kissed.

With a selfless drive we fought
Just for a day of total freedom,
It was what we so heartily sought,
A holy freedom of St. Peter's dome.

It was a gorgeous fragrant rose
Surrounded with lackluster prose.

The Truth is So Abrupt

The truth is so abrupt
After it gets unveiled,
A scandal may erupt,
There is no bail from hate,
The brittle peace is dumped,
The friendships are derailed.

Our constant silence is a sin,
No one can ever lose or win,
It is forever vanity or pride,
We run from truth,
But cannot hide.

The shadows loom,
We fight the gloom,
We try until we faint.

But only one becomes a saint.

The Truth of History Erased

The truth of history erased,
The lies of wars embraced.

I walked, flanked by the graves,
I ran among the stars and crosses,
Above the haven for the braves,
Across their wins and bitter losses.

Wars often come, wars go,
Peace wanders in between,
Nobody stops after a draw,
Nobody stops after a win.

When lose, why can't we stop?
As in Vietnam it was a blunder
For those who reigned on top,
But death for those
Who followed under.

War stopped on Earth,
Time stopped above,
Peace died at birth,
Died as a loveless dove.

The lies of wars embraced,
The truth of history erased.

The Truth Unearthed

I curbed my sense of guilt,
In vain, I virtually built
A newer, better paradigm.
I tried to bolt and solder
A user-friendly, quiet order,
But ran out of costly time.

In war, there was no man
Who didn't know fear,
A few were terrified and ran,
We readjusted our gear.

Being a fighter and a poet
I knew two trades of man
In times of war and peace,
Keep living 'til you blow it,
Sing sweetened serenades
Just like a rooster to a hen,
And write your masterpieces.

We use our long-lasting lives
To learn what we supposed
To know right from our births.
We wasted days and nights
Catching the bloody knives
Of tyrannies we all opposed,
Shielding the truth unearthed.

Life was a head rolling competition,
The second mouse got the cheese,
We craved the Golden Fleece
But missed the forest for the trees.

The Twins have Left

Two towers-twins,
Two preys of sins.
I brought two flowers,
For burials of towers.

A heavy silence of the void,
Magnetic hearts of sorrows,
Teardrops of the destroyed,
The past to our tomorrows.

The twins have left,
They walked away,
We watched the dire theft,
We couldn't save the prey.

Inseparable in life,
Inseparable in death,
They failed to win the strive,
We caught their final breath.

I saw the heinous plume,
My memories still fight
Two shafts of gloom,
Their awful final flight.

Their souls were touched
Before they went above,
The sky was sadly scratched
By tortured twins of our love.

The Underground Skies

I want to see the underground skies
Where our laughter fights the cries.

A few remains of our firm
Resistance,
A few persisting bits of our
Existence
Shatter the monolith of our
Addictions,
Demolish solid walls of our
Convictions.

I want to search under the hood,
I don't want pills, I want my food,
I am not a criminal released on bail,
I am not a racing boat without a sail,
I am not a cat forever gray at night,
I want to climb the beams of light,
I want to see the depth of the abyss,
Blistering summers, not the springs,
I had reserved a lovely room in bliss
To see the sinners with two wings.

Our world was dark and boundless
Enigma,
Before His hands were marked with
Stigma,
Before He fell into the fiery abyss,
Before He soared to Father's bliss.

Today, I wouldn't have
To slide to burning hell
To see our seven mortal sins;
Today, I use my ears and eyes,
And see them here in paradise;
They are living sensibly and well.

The Unforgiven Sin

It was a necessary end,
He fell on his own sword,
Contained and free;
He was my bosom friend,
I've heard his final word,
"Agree to disagree".

The great conductor
Of our veiled desires,
Unwilling benefactor
Of our daily paradise,
A sentimental bard
Of yet unknown art.

He went for broke,
No one would let him win,
It was an agonizing yoke,
It was the unforgiven sin.

Above the red vineyard,
Under the scorching sun,
Wrapped in the yellow sky;
But as our conscience guard,
He pulled that merciless gun.
The fallen angel let him die.

The Urge of My Desire

The urge of my desire
Set up my heart on fire,
I couldn't kill the flame,
I am the one to blame.

I can't forget
The fools and petty liars,
The sorrows of betrayals,
The spectacles of fires,
The puzzles of the trails;
The great inferno of sunset.

The anxious firefighters
Fending off the smoke,
I see a few all-nighters,
Some cry, some choke.

The old burned bridge
Still smoking in the air,
I am sliding from the ridge
Into the pit of my despair.

The friendships reach their ends,
Life slowly fades and disappears,
There are no enemies or friends,
Unwillingly, I outlived my peers.

I hear a quiet sigh
Of our mute farewell,
I hear a loud cry
Of the emerging hell.

The Wall of Worries

The lightning's painful blade
Slashed our harmless skies,
It was a blazing vicious raid
Of sheepish evil in disguise.

Too late for dances,
Too early for a kiss;
I take my unrealistic chances
I am standing in a line to bliss.

I hear the symphonies of guns,
I hear the rhapsodies of shells,
Corps de ballet of ammunition
Supplies a primadonna AK-47.
I stand the heat of many suns,
I bring the drought to the wells,
I see the artistry of a mortician
Carving a staircase to heaven.

I downed a few vodka glasses,
I want to see the happy ends,
My silent farewell glances
Touched faces of my friends,
I heard their heartfelt stories,
I climbed the wall of worries.

Too early for a goodbye kiss,
I am still in the pursuit of bliss.

The War is Over

The war is over.
There's no dialogue
Among a therapeutic beauty
Of everchanging skies
And dying warriors on duty,
Forever closing tired eyes.

The war is over,
And yet, my torturous hangover
Brings in the middle of the night,
The reminiscences of every fight.

The war is over.
I crave disharmony of colors,
I crave cacophony of sounds,
I never strive to find a balance
Between a tempest and a lull,
Between forte and weakness,
Between extravagant and dull,
Amid my health and sickness.

The war is over.
I am not drinking in the pubs,
I float in a societal limelight
Along casinos and strip clubs,
Among each Freudian delight:
Pulsating silhouettes
Of stripping tender girls,
The young enticing pets
In counterfeited pearls.

The war is over,
There is no dialogue
Between a metaphoric beauty
Of everchanging skies,
And our warriors, killed on duty,
That closed their hopeless eyes.

The Warmth of Judas' Kiss

Conniving friend,
A treacherous affair,
There is no end
To my incurable despair.

Serenity of a morning breeze,
The pain of a brutal treason,
The warmth of the Judas kiss,
Must have a higher reason.

Those who are close to you,
Possess much sharper knives,
The innocence of morning dew
Can't cleanse their sinful lives.

Wild beasts of my nightmares
Ravenously perform their best,
After my fight with evil's heirs,
I shall return into my cozy nest.

Conniving friend,
A treacherous affair,
I see the gleaming end,
And tombstones of despair.

While most of us are clueless,
I thank God's chosen Judas,
Your kiss shaped resurrection,
Created bliss and the abyss,
Led every sin to its perfection.

The Wheels of Time

I've been to ancient Bethlehem,
I've seen the brightest star,
I've seen a cradle of the lamb,
I've seen the wise men from afar.

Army invasion
Can be resisted,
But not a great idea
If a good time arrived;
For this exact occasion,
I am ready, I am two-fisted:
I will not try to sing Ave Maria,
I'll fight tooth and nail for the revived.

The foam was blown off the beer,
The sea of pessimism looks clear.
I hear the deafness of my soul,
I see the darkness of my dreams.
I watch the wheels of time still roll
Much faster than it seems.

It's a time of empty gestures,
It's a time of useless words,
It's a time of crooked ventures,
It's a time of rusty, futile swords.

Malicious ignorance
Of modern vandals
Looks like a meager dance
Between two burning candles,
Like doors without handles,
No ins, no outs,
Roads to nowhere are endless
They have no maps or routs.

Choked by unleashed plutocracy
I tried to think and breathe,
Surrounded by timid mediocracy,
I earned a tombstone or a wreath.

I am forbidden to forget,
I am forbidden to forgive,
Only a meaningful reset
May cure my will to live.

The Winds of Autumn Were so Cold

The winds of autumn were so cold,
The grove of maple trees was old,
I hit the bottom; I was a fallen leaf,
I was a sinner; I was a thief…

I flung the dice, it rolled
Into the end of a sad story;
I am numb, my soul is sold,
There is no shame or glory.

I stopped the endless strife,
I threw away my troubled life,
I jumped from the rocky cliff
Into the sea of grief.

Those whom I leave behind,
Don't judge, try to be kind.
Unbearable was pain,
I didn't want to live insane.

The Word Birthed Our World

The word that birthed our hazy world
Perpetuity invites our desire to learn,
Ignites our imagination and creativity,
Then builds our science and the arts.

Countless artists enlighten obscurity,
The times endure pains of an elation;
An artist must be kicked to breathe
As a newborn slapped by a midwife.

The arts become exuberant miracles
Overpowering the swamps of apathy,
Demoralizing the towers of antipathy,
Streaming into the hearts of humans,
Entering unnourished, hungry souls,
Then turning into the waterfalls of joy,
Running into the ocean of knowledge.

Our knowledge brings creative doubts,
These doubts open up the other worlds,
Those worlds already learned the word.

There Are No Antidotes

There are no antidotes
To senseless violence,
They slash our throats,
Our songs are silenced.

We can no longer bear
This dreadful nightmare:
The angels never fall;
They simply soar
Into the underground sky,
And take a curtain call.
We don't applaud, we cry,
We roar.
We tag a chosen guide,
Our mass illusions float;
The rising bloody tide
Sunk every elder boat.

Why don't we thwart
Our fear of seeing?
Is there a higher court
That recognizes our being?
There is a darker angel
That ascends
To count our sins.
There is another angel
That descends
To count our wins,

The happy end:
A tiny yellow yolk
Hangs in the sky;
Breakfast in bed.

There Is No Answer

I don't ignore my premonitions,
But look at the reality instead;
At times, it is a comedy,
At times, it is a tragedy,
And only our timeless missions
Bring to the tables daily bread.

It is not a bit surprising:
The moon stopped rolling,
The sun stopped rising,
The skies are falling;
I realized it in a minute,
Eternity was in it…

I saw a huge inviting sign,
My curiosity and hunger
Pushed the door;
I sensed the smells of bacon,
Boiled spinach, and fish fat
Infused with a diluted Irish beer;
My mood was civil yet austere,
I went into a bar avoiding a long line,
Where each was staring at the floor,
And hardly mumbling this and that.

Don't ask me anything,
I have no clue; there is no answer.
Last night, I brought a wedding ring
To a delightful pole dancer.

I used all arrows from my quiver,
My poetry helped us understand ourselves.
I didn't pull the classics from the dusty shelves,
I didn't try to enter twice into the same old river.

There is No Letter "WE"

We cheerfully fly
With our friends,
We hover in the sky,
And wish it never ends.

Two lonely birds,
Two lonely trees,
Two lonely nerds
Across the seas.

There is a letter "I",
There is a letter "U",
The endless sky,
You look for me,
I look for you;
For instance,
There is no letter "WE",
The distance
Isolating you from me.

I know,
You will say qui, qui,
Our hearts will glow
If there is a letter "WE".

Two lonely souls,
Not our faults…

There is no Paradise on Earth

I wander like a child
Between the legs of time,
Somebody tries to hide,
The others try to climb.

The calendar drops pages
On my survival's grimy floor,
I cash them as the wages
For my seductive sprawl;
I simply risk my better days,
I want to exit from this maze.

I stir the sediment or so it seems
In a lethargic bottle of my dreams,
And in the fortress of my home,
I gulp my beer and slurp the foam.

I didn't write my will,
I didn't try to fool my fate,
If there is any thrill,
It always comes too late.

Where are those dreamy castles,
My illusory quest from birth?
I only see the nasty daily hustles,
There is no paradise on Earth…

There is no Victory

There is no victory in sight,
Hopes fade; the choir still sings,
A jingoistic language cannot fight,
The goddess Nike lost both wings.

The seed of doubts lost its husk,
If there's any victory, it's Pyrrhic,
Dead soldiers melt into the dusk,
I carve my melancholic lyric.

Take lessons from the past,
The future may not come,
I hear another blast…
A son won't see his Mom.

We did return into the past,
We re-enact an old Vietnam,
Iraq, Afghanistan will last
As long as we are numb.

I watched the news,
Another child has died;
Another deathly blues,
Another mother cried...

There Was a Warning Sign

I marched my marriage trail,
I gathered fruits of my defeat,
I could no longer bear the heat
And noxious toxins of betrayal.

A year already passed
Like a dark shadow
Of a dying love.
My wounded memory caressed
A parting kiss you tried to blow,
Without even taking off a glove.

Another marriage fell apart
To justify our statistics' chart.

I fell to six feet under,
I climbed the wall of worry
To hear a booming thunder,
To face the light of glory.
I curled from wrong to right
To thread a single needle,
I went into the blinding light
To solve that lifelong riddle.

I tried to catch a falling knife,
Let fall to a butcher's block,
I sadly lost this uphill strife,
And landed on the rock.

There was a warning sign:
"Your time had flowed,
Your life had crested,
You crossed the line,
Your body will be towed,
Your soul will be arrested.

Hard times will never pass
Like sand in the hourglass,
The stars will never glow
And sparkle like a virgin snow."

There was No One Around

My morbid deep inertia,
A beautiful eternal void,
Is like a rug from Persia
Above a couch of Dr. Freud.

I am chasing my own shadows
As if I am returning to my past,
Where sunrise never goes
As yesterdays have passed.

The prophets and auspicious minds
Live in successive layers of tomorrows,
Although, a calculation never finds
All those who never leave the burrows.

Last night, I only saw the moon,
Last night, I only heard the blues,
No stars, only a heartfelt tune
Forgotten even by my muse.
Last night, it was a twilight zone,
There was no one around,
I took my promenade alone,
I was in my nirvana drowned.

I always envied laughing babies,
I am on track to start my life anew
Against those no's and maybes,
For all the yes's I could chew.

Sunrise was bright,
No clock to beat,
No one to fight
To get a seat.

There was no one around,
I was in freedom drowned.

.

These Wars Swipe Our Souls

While we are dying in the fights,
These wars swipe our souls;
Warmongers watch the horrid sights,
Meanwhile ascending in the polls.

Birds of the plume
We flock into that thrill,
Inhale the noxious fume,
And plead for a refill.

We reenact the days of gladiators
Killed and devoured by the lions,
We fight like mindless alligators
Converged into a forged alliance.

Our leaders pull us off the tables,
We die. Come back in filthy boxes.
They ably imitate the crazy foxes,
And write about war heroes fables.

Bigmouthed trash,
Don't sweat in fear,
Wars make them cash,
They screen their cheer.

Newly converted whores
Wrapped in the US flags,
Start their atrocious wars,
To watch us coming in the bags.

They Flaunt my Shaggy Face

They flaunt my shaggy face
On the "Most Wanted" posters,
I am in a hell-raising race,
I ride the human roller-coasters.

I am waiting for an arraignment,
Handcuffed in downtown court
On charges of engagement
With a lavish life I can't afford:
My day has no tomorrow,
I cannot pay, but borrow,
I love, eat, drink, and write,
I meet a friend or pick a fight.

I am completely guiltless
Of this insufferable crime,
But I am harshly punished:
My thoughts are wingless,
My verses have no rhyme,
My innovations vanished.

I am insane from time to time,
And mulishly commit this crime
As if I want to clip my wings;
I bought a pair of wedding rings.

They Will Not Whisper Verses

First laughing days of spring,
A glass of great champagne,
We'd rather smile and sing,
Healing our agonizing pain.

You were an island
In the sea of life,
You were a garland
I was a falling knife.

You were evasive
As a fragile dream,
I was aggressive
As a laser beam.

I would declare a war,
You would deny a fight,
Sheer ecstasy of our affair
Fills our haven to its shore,
Our bodies clothed in light,
Our souls stripped bare.

The tired spring passed by,
The summer said goodbye,
The autumn came n' went,
The icy winter left its scent,
Another perky sunny spring
Has come and wants to sing.

The end of spring in our life,
We're two worn-out horses,
I want new seasons to arrive,
They'll descend to our nook,
They'll gently whisper verses
To empty pages of my book.

This Is My Prayer,

This is my last desire,
I paid the heinous fare,
Don't let me burn in fire.

My brain remembers
The pain, the screams,
The torture chambers,
The suicidal dreams.

The endless hallways,
Eternity of nights and days,
No hope, but faith and love
As if I didn't have enough.

Descend from the cloud,
Bring wings, teach me to fly,
I walk the burning grounds,
I am not a seagull in the sky.

There is no color in my pain
To paint the freezing rain,
I crawled across the dirt,
I screamed, nobody heard.

My wishes flow in the skies,
Visible to millions of eyes,
I hear their tearful farewell,
I am still in hell…

Through a Keyhole

It was a long and sleepless night.
A dawn was standing at the door.
Was it a love from the first sight?
Was it a quiet peace after a war?

I am a stubborn sturdy tree
Streaming from a wrinkle-crack
Belonging to a boring tired face
Of a cliff wiped daily by the sea.

My calm equilibrium reflects
My twofold personalities,
Injected with graffiti texts,
And studded with banalities.

I'd rather stay anonymous and quiet,
I'd rather be a wise observer;
And yet I'd rather be arrested in a riot
Than work as a submissive server.

I face my external pressures
With principled defiance,
And disregard their measures
That substitute my art with science.

I cherish my foreign outsider role,
Marching to my own tune and beat;
I wouldn't look through a keyhole
To see where both ends meet.

Life isn't a constant Christmas time,
Most great things have no rhyme.

To B.

You are the morning breeze,
I am flying through the mist,
You are the acrobat on a trapeze,
I am a hunger at the end of feast.

The secret golden key,
The glee of your September
Opens the cage and lets me flee,
You are a spark of glowing ember.

I am a painted bird,
Red as a drop of blood,
In trinity you're the third,
You're the blooming bud.

After this night,
The sun shall rise,
Your beauty is the light,
I swim and drown in your eyes.

You had the magic key
From golden cages of September.
You opened them and set us free
like sparks of still glowing amber.

You are a morning breeze,
I live in anguish as a failing beast,
I am a lonely acrobat on a trapeze,
I am still hungry at the end of the feast.

To Beth

A Russian icon of your face
Melts modestly and hides
Behind the curtains' lace,
Behind the stripes of blinds.

I'll walk over the tired sorrow,
The lights are off on Sundays,
I'll meet someone tomorrow,
I'll fly in ecstasy on Mondays.

Deep anguish of my oath,
Obscurity and pain of grief,
I am a stranger to them both,
I am a swirling autumn leaf.

I hid my sorrows on the shelf,
Tonight, I dance, drink wine,
I hope back home I will be fine,
But what if I only tease myself?

The Russian icon of your face
Gleams through the gentle lace.

Triumphant Nike

The darkest night falls
Into the palms of dusk,
My inner demon calls,
But I won't lose my husk.

The history repeats itself,
New tragedies destroy
A vaudeville of life,
Old comedies are hiding
On a dusty shelf
From battles of a modern
Strife.

Dense shadows of these
Days,
Loom fearlessly above my
Nights,
My sleepless, needy body
Craves
To fall into a self-indulging
"Garden of delights".

Great Bosch entices my
Nomadic mind,
Although, rejects my soul,
As if the blind cruelly leads
The blind
Into a more attractive hole.

Only the ancient ice
Resists the sun of springs,
I merely close my eyes,
Triumphant Nike lost her
Wings.

Two Clouds Argue in the Lake

The yellow-orange trees
Above the verdant field,
Two clouds argue in the lake,
Who's lighter than the breeze,
A secret envelope is sealed,
New hurricane is in the make.

Blue birds of wishes flew,
They landed on your day,
The autumns giving you
What winters take away.

Two clouds argue in the lake,
New hurricane is in the make.

Two Murky Windows

Whether it's an evenness of equinox
Or a long-distanced solstice's icebox,
I'd rather die and rest in peace
Than live forever on my knees;
I planned to shine my dirty hoofs
Before I meet my old creator,
That hope is hanging in a noose
Above our planet's long equator.

I climbed the wall of worry,
I am in a nosebleed territory,
I watch the nations from the sky;
They fight, nobody wins; it is a tie.

Nevertheless, the low hanging fruit
Was seized by a determent demon,
By such a nasty and conniving brute,
Who has deposited his tainted semen
In every desperate or a hungry womb.
Thus, we are his heirs; we are in bloom.

The light from a table lamp
Lies like an orange on the floor,
Or like a yellow postage-stamp;
Too bad, I don't write letters anymore.
I am just clinking glasses with my peers,
We are drunk and laughing into tears;
The Russian vodka won the race,
The Irish whiskey took a second place.

Two murky windows of my soul,
Both of my hangover's foggy eyes,
Won't ever help me to regain control
Over the jolly demons in disguise.

Two wedding rings,
Two total strangers,
Two pairs of wings,
Two flying angels,
Two birds in bliss,
Two naked souls
Above the trees,
Above the walls.

Another short affair,
Another losing hand,
Another parted pair,
Another tragic end.

Two lonely strangers,
Two fallen angels…

Unavoidable Endzone

A naughty morning breeze
Wakes memories of yesterdays;
In premonition of a strong espresso
That starts my crooked daily maze
With its intriguing aromatic tease,
And ancient games of quid pro quo.

These ritualistic daily habits
Deliver coffee and the news;
These necessary and sufficient tidbits
Mold my nobody-cares-to-know views.

The young do what they want,
The elder don't;
The elder calm; they know truth,
They simply miss their youth.

Another autumn passed;
I'm standing at the edge
Of a slowly looming overcast;
The cranes are flying lined in a wedge
Above our Mother Nature's paradigm…
I'm a dreamy poet; a dozen for a dime.

I have removed specifics,
I have converted life into ambiguities,
And bravely jumped into linguistics,
As if I raked my microscopic gratuities
Into an unavoidable endzone…

Is it a milestone or my tombstone?

Under a Wounded Sky

I didn't travel overseas
In search of paradise,
I paid for a striptease
Of angels in disguise.

I stood on yet unknown earth,
I held the weightless skies,
I cast a see-through shadow.
It was a moment of rebirth,
I whispered my goodbyes
To everything I used to know.

I'm not interested in things,
I'd rather study their relations,
I place eternity of springs
Above our futile declarations.

I dwell under a wounded sky,
Pierced by the flying cranes,
At times, when clouds cry,
I wash my seven sins in rains.

I was alone before,
I'm alone today,
I'll be alone tomorrow.
I write,
No one begs an encore,
At night,
All cats are gray,
A poet has to die to glow.

I'll reach the end of skies,
I'll touch the end of land,
I'll die with opened eyes
To see a marching band.

Uninvited Guest

Against my will I am in the race;
It's not my place, there is no thrill.

I am a gun already drawn,
I am a disaffected, crazy artist,
I am in pursuit of the unknown,
I am a resuscitated John the Baptist,
I am the one who knew the word,
I have baptized the future of this world.

Even a fool may learn;
Nobody gauged my wit
By giving love I didn't want to earn,
By blowing out a dry wick that wasn't lit.
Nobody gauged my strength
By measuring stupidity of others;
I simply keep the crowds at the length,
And no one cares, and no one bothers.

I try to cloak my life in happiness of light,
I am still wandering from coast to coast,
I try to keep the sun above my head;
My needle didn't drag the thread,
Reality didn't support my quest;
I realized, I am not a host,
I am an uninvited guest.

Because I learned the truth:
Only the forests lie;
I am the one who knows why;
It is because nobody sees
The forest for the trees.
Only the blind desire a tease.

Vicious Stones

We judge; God may forgive,
The Book: "We are his clones,
We take, we seldom give,
We cast our vicious stones".

We've been here twice,
We turned about face,
And walked our own ways,
And paid a twofold price.

Tomorrows were so bright and vast,
But morphed into a joyless desert,
Our history creates a murky present,
Described as glory of the Holy past.

We stroll the Periodic Table
Amid the faceless elements
Cast like the gambling dice;
We learn this tiresome fable
Of predetermined payments
That open gates of paradise.

When silence fills our rooms,
We blame our idle ears;
We are as innocent as grooms,
We still shed our shameful tears.

Most likely, we are born to sleep
Yet seldom die in our own bed;
We welcome our death and weep
Then fly into the skies instead.

We All Are Guests on Earth

We all are guests on Earth,
We hear it from our birth,
Some mavens even say,
We have to justify our stay.

On Sundays, every week
I look into a hollow sky
And turn the other cheek
Or plea an eye for an eye.
It's time to make my mind,
Stay merciless or be kind.

I'm not a giant
On the feet of clay,
I wouldn't crumble,
I'd rather sway,
I whistle past the boneyard,
My skeletons rest
Six feet under,
At dawn,
I'm a warrior diehard,
At dusk,
I'm fearful of thunder,
In pride I want to win,
In vain I long for glory,
It's just a lukewarm sin,
It's just at times a chance
To say I'm sorry.

I will unfurl my sail,
The winds will blow,
On journey to
The Holy Grail,

I hope the Lord
Controls the flow.

The wise men wail,
You'll live and die,
I try and often fail,
But never fail to try.

We All Take Turns

The trees die standing tall,
The men collapse or sprawl,
Only the angels live forever,
Good luck in that endeavor.

I am a jailbird of aloneness,
A victim of a public solitude
That angels brought upon us;
I am ready for a higher altitude.

I walk along my gloomy street,
Hiding in its chaotic shadows,
And asking for a trick-or-treat.
I ask for poetry, get only prose.

I walk along my gloomy street,
And hear my never written songs
Piercing the silence of defeat,
For anonymity no one yet longs.

The riddles of tainted prosecutors
Are solved with a surprising help
Of quantum superfast computers;
While our old devices noisily yelp
Over trapped ions and new qubits,
Split like in a painting by a cubist.

A dull monotony of my worn-out life
Will be destroyed by a new strife,
Or by an entirely unfamiliar truth,
By a deeply nihilistic cultured youth.

We Are Breaking Bread

The burdens of the civilized
Are not to comfort the offenders,
We fight, we won't be brutalized
By vicious armed bystanders.

Enchanting tales of war,
Persuading, yet puerile,
Breaking into my open door,
Motley surrealist and vile.

Wars don't intrigue me anymore,
I need a few expertly able hands
To play the bitter requiem to war,
I wrote for brassy marching bands.

Regrettably, war isn't ending
Under bloodthirsty overcasts,
My poetry does genre-bending
In the pursuit of peace that lasts.

I am looking for a precious thread
Belonging to elusive Golden fleece,
In vain, yet we are breaking bread,
It's hard but we're making peace.
We buried hatchets with our foes.
There are no winners in this war,
We use our heads not elbows
In this affectionate esprit de corps.

Life is a mysterious unopened bud.
The Holy Grail leaked like a sieve,
I didn't get a drop of wine or blood
When I unearthed that costly cup.
I gladly and full heartedly believe,
Till someone rudely wakes me up.

We Are Religious Enough to Hate

A real sailor is a fatalist,
My name is always on that list,
A sailor never learns to swim,
He trusts in fate and Seraphim.

He doesn't go up to face the end,
He doesn't fly; he only goes down,
St. Andrew knows where he went,
He'll watch the stars and drown.

I love the hookers and the sailors,
I love brave soldiers and strippers,
The rest of us are silent failures,
The gliding swans without ripples.

I've leafed again the Book of Life,
My heroes die; the cowards thrive.
I've read a page after a page,
I locked my demons in the cage.

Our innocence falls for the bait,
Our prides will never stop to bluff,
We are religious enough to hate,
But not enough to love…

We Docked at the D'Orsey

These days I'm living large,
I travel on a comfy barge,
Pont Neuf arches ahead,
A heaven for the artsy-mad,
We docked at the d'Orsey,
Rocked by the river's play.

I've heard a movie maven,
"We'll always have Paris",
If this is not a real heaven,
Then show me what is.

Old waiters recognize
My polished presence,
For that I paid a price,
They liked my presents.

Time fails to hide
Our wrinkled skins,
Years left behind,
We lose, time wins.

In front of me a wall,
Behind, a broken life,
Inside, a littered soul,
I am trying to survive.

I doubt while in France,
If I'll ever have a sense,
This is my farewell visit
Into the capital of lights,
The final time to see it
Before infinity of nights.

We Had a Pause

The moon calmed our planet Earth,
In the meantime, eclipsed the sun;
We had a pause to find our berth,
But we'll miss the light of dawn.

I didn't notice it before,
Even the doors have eyes;
They watched, I went to war,
I heard their heartfelt sighs;
A few years later, I did return
With scratches here and there;
This time it is my turn
To be attentive, generous and fair.

I limit colors of my dreams
To shades of black and white;
These days, my future seems
Utterly inviting, warm, and bright.

I woke in a sentimental mood,
Within the remnants of my childhood
I found the almighty Prince of Light.
He led me from a lackluster wrong
Into eternity of a glowing right.

We Have Returned as One

John's head fell on the tray,
Last song of a dying swan,
We went divided far away,
We have returned as one.

Tomorrow came too soon,
The ugly vultures landed,
They took my silver spoon,
In vain they tried to bend it.

I laughed or grieved
Behind locked doors,
Then I was sieved
Through heinous wars.

New expectations bring
The same unending cry,
I need a frigging drink,
My lonesome soul is dry.

When mothers know best,
Please, get some rest,
When fathers know best,
Young man, go west.

To those who know best,
Wars started by the goons,
Destroyed our cushy nests
Under the passing moons.

They circle by my barn,
It wouldn't fit their guns,
If I'll hear goddamn or darn,
They'll never see new suns.

We went divided far away,
We have returned as one.

We Heard His Last Goodbye

His heart is flying in the past,
His soul is flying in the future,
Both cast the saddest shadows
On our lives without peace,
On our days and nights of war,
Connected with a bloody suture.

He pulled the fast drive lever,
He said, "I will be young forever,"
To his beloved crying bride
And plunged into a war to fight;
He never lied…
Our leaders reached their goal;
Forever young he died,
Forever young remains his soul.

He kept his word;
So many moons passed by,
We heard his last goodbye
From a much better world.

Our elected leeches,
Our elected whores,
Our chosen bitches
Still lie and dodder,
Still take the floors,
Deliver speeches…
While we are used
As cannon fodder
In their futile wars.

We Knew the Edge of Pain

Your life is dawn-to-dusk,
My life is dusk-to-dawn,
We peel the futile husk
Until the thrill has gone.

You're bedding down
For the night,
I'm rushing downtown
For the light.

We knew the edge of pain,
We built the hedge on love,
We spitefully fought in vain,
Even enough wasn't enough.

Without shields of bodyguards
Our precious songs of hearts
Were dedicated to distress
And self-complacency. Unless,
We ran away from boredom
Of the Kafkaesque grotesque,
Of cute, but morbid whoredom
Into the harbored humoresque.

We roamed through our tunes,
We sang our luscious songs,
Under the cozy hazy moons,
Above the rights and wrongs.

We Miss

We drum and march,
We overlook the beat,
We waste our years,
We burn the witches,
We make ends meet,
We sprint from fears,
Run from the crunch,
Embrace the leeches,
We miss, we never hit,
We miss those routes
Of a scientific solitude
And a high-wire fiction
Amid the daring bouts
Of a hilarious prelude
To human jurisdiction.

We Never Have to Bark

My strange nightmare:
I walk across the blaze,
My fortune sheers
Under your fiery glare.
I cloak my face
With salty tears.

I am a guardian angel
Above the rising billows;
I am a sympathetic ranger
Above the weeping willows.

I fall and crawl,
I stand and fall,
I climb and fly,
I walk…
I hover in the sky,
I am a red-tailed hawk…

A red sunset sent its adieu,
Decisions come at nights;
I am here ahead of you,
We have to end our fights.

Some wander in the dark,
Some kiss the ugly frogs,
Why do we have to bark?
For that we have our dogs.

We are not vandals,
We have to make amends,
We cannot burn our candles
From both ends.

We Never Learned to Fly

A red-tailed hawk
Fell from the sky,
He'll learn to walk,
We'll learn to fly.

Love's sassy poison ivy,
The passion of last night,
We mention rather wryly
About our shared delight.

The legions of small birds
Flaunt voices on the trees,
The chirping careless girls
Remind me fallen leaves.

These fallen leaves
No one remembers,
The rains and tears
Of our Novembers.

The boat of life
Rocks in the flow,
We must survive
We have to row,
Fate raked us all,
The boat is full,
No aim, no goal,
Each is a fool.

We never want to rest,
Devour countless miles,
We climb the Everest,
As pinnacle of our lives,

The fluffy flakes of snow
Melt on your rosy cheeks,
Only a long stone's throw
And we'll reach the peak.

A proud red-tailed hawk
Descended from the sky,
He learned to walk,
We never learned to fly.

We Play the Same Old Tune

The sheets of music
Are the same for all,
We play the same old tune,
Why do some run into the wall,
While others soar on the balloon?

When I was prematurely born,
Nobody fetched a silver spoon,
An angel didn't blow the horn,
Even the night forgot to moon.

A creepy foreword to my life
Predicted victories of failures,
I entered a blood-thirsty strife
With mysteries of devil's lures.

I saw his finger on the scale,
We fought; I didn't want to fail.

The deck was stacked,
My horse was in the race,
I had no time to go back,
And pulled a lucky ace.

I did my best, I played and won,
My friends have left. I am alone.

From eight to five,
The cutthroat daily glee
Of my exhilarating life
Plays nasty tricks on me.

I watch nightmares at night
And bark yet at the other moon,
The dullness gifts me a delight,
It leases me a smile at noon.

We Polish Precious Gifts

We walk a forest of our past,
Among the lowland swamps,
Our engagements never last,
We leave, the future stomps.

We open envelopes,
To see tomorrows,
With telescopes
We alter our hopes,
With microscopes
We cure our sorrows.

The terror of confusion
We kindly named a life,
The kingdom of illusion
We named a death,
Please, drink and thrive,
Don't hold your breath.

Time-bomb defused
As many other ploys,
Infinity descended,
We're still confused,
Our frail lives rejoice,
Our deaths offended.

The winds of change
Bring light tomorrows,
We iron on the bench
The robes of sorrows.

We polish precious gifts,
We punish, God forgives.

We Send the Wreaths

We fight and thrive,
A few young soldiers
Play soccer outside,
None of them dares
To say who is alive,
And who has died.

We're forever under Him,
We all will enter bliss,
Because His whim
Froze the abyss.

We rarely say goodbye,
Just "see you later";
The moons pass by,
And fall into a crater;
According to the myths
We send the wreaths.

New war already looms,
A shaky peace won't last,
I craved to see the moons,
I didn't want to see the past.

At nights, I see those years,
Unfortunately soaked in red,
And bring my fallen peers
To break my daily bread.

We Share a Quiet Sigh

A heavy thundercloud
Brews slowly overhead,
The hearts still pound,
The hearts of our dead.

We hear the vicious sounds,
Death flies over the bounds,
The Satan reaps the fruit,
Our goodness is his loot.

We crawl into the room
Of our bitter sorrows,
We close the windows,
We shut the doors,
We run into the womb
From our tomorrows,
From bliss of rainbows,
From our tour de force.

We walk the paths
Across the grieves,
Across the wraths,
Across the myths.

We walk into the fight,
Into the feisty night,
We share a quiet sigh
With those who die.

There are no hymns,
There are no odes,
Only the sour themes
On our poetic roads.

We Share our Daily Bread

Those moons long passed,
Somebody carved in stone:
"You want to go fast,
You walk alone,
You want to go far,
We walk together."
Time lulls my sleeping car,
It trembles like a feather,
I count endless miles,
I am coming from afar
To sleep in your dark eyes.

I am weary of goodbyes
When lives are wrecked,
I hear the saddest sighs
When boats are decked.

I veer along fast cars,
I'm soaking in the bars,
My wounds are deep,
I drink, I scarcely sleep.

I pass through ancient
Foreign Lands,
Too many broken lives
Dwelled here and bled,
I meet amazing friends,
I shake their hands
In every celebrated dive,
We share our daily bread.

We Slept in a Motel

Don't wait for friends,
No one will come,
Just meet the ends
And stay alive.
Loves awfully numb,
Don't dive.

A pretty girl became
My travel agent,
She wasted my vacation
On a redneck Riviera,
Got fat on slimy gumbos
Of a dimwitted Cajun,
Then wept through her
Mascara.

I put my hammer down
And quickly moved ahead,
She kept me for a clown,
But I was thinking of a bed.

Dull means were justified
By shiny ends,
Life waited for a drought
To start its rainy trends,
To wash my doubts out.

We slept in a motel,
I never kiss and tell.

We Tango in the Sky

What is the turning world
For those who are insane,
Who don't enjoy the chord
Of dancing tango in the rain?

Our dancing bodies tremble,
Cast shadows on the wall,
I lead you with my hand,
You are so elegantly tender,
We pivot, sway and stroll,
As if we're one until the end.

The heartless mannequins
Destroy our daytime worlds,
The tango reigns at night,
The openhearted harlequins
Bring tango-loving hordes
To dance milongas of delight.

Bandoneons play
Under the quiet sky,
I can no longer stay,
I have to learn to fly.

The tango lovers fly
Over the Milky Way,
We tango in the sky
After we pass away.

We Used a Groovy Slang

A piercing night
Wears its tuxedo
As a common trend,
The lights are bright,
Enough to meet a foe,
Enough to see a friend.

We enter colleges of life,
Take courses of the street,
We learn to bravely strive,
We learn to be discreet.

We used a groovy slang
When Eric Carmen sang:
"Lovemaking was for fun,
Those days have gone."

The bright mosaics
Of those misty dusks,
The songs of dawns
And young desires,
The psychedelic
Streaming waves
Brought sheer insanity
On altars of sunrise.

We sowed, youth will reap
The fruit of healthy nihilism,
We wonder if disasters leap
Over the path of cataclysm.

The darkened narrow runway
Of life's expected daily stress
Morphs into a fast highway
Of our frightening regress.

We Watch Firsthand

The sky loves land,
The union of true equals;
We shily watch firsthand
The mystery of sequels.

Two stars, one hope,
Two czars, one rope.

The sky is everywhere:
West, south, east or north,
Lands also dwell up there,
Sways back and forth,
Looks like a love affair
For what it's worth.

These are two flames,
They burn each other,
They play the games:
The fights don't bother
Their self-inflicted pains.

The tired winter's throw
Can't hide fast streams
Amid the melting snow,
A hurried water gleams.

During the springs
Land loves the skies;
No wedding rings,
No wedding pies.

While Empty Pages Wait

I live, I cannot stop, I cannot fall asleep,
I have to be on top while others weep,
I am a shark circling the bogus bait,
I swim while empty pages wait.

The tears of rain fall on my face,
I hug myself; it is a very sad embrace,
I'd rather hug my muse, my lifelong love,
Her guidance I forever use fits like a glove.

I had to cross the bridge,
Being a prisoner of time;
My heart is in the fridge,
Cold is a perfect paradigm.

I must unlock the door,
And let my talents flee,
Into the joy galore
To share my glee.

My masquerade is blown,
I am back to vicious races,
I throw everything I own
Into my critics faces.

I live, I write, I cannot stop,
My muse advices, be on top.

While I am Still a Man

The heartless sober clouds
Buried the vodka-drunken sun;
It is too late for thank you bouts,
I tossed a burger on a bun.

A cute redhaired bartender,
Wearing a dusty military gear;
She is a boozer and offender,
She pours me Guinness beer.

A trendy purple dotty polish
Shows off her hawkish nails;
She's serving sex as garnish
When every other effort fails.

My endless leisure
Rhymes with seizure:
If I will get another DUI,
I will be calmly hung to dry.

The wolves are fed,
The sheep are still alive;
A total paradigm, no mess;
I do continuously guess
From a weekdays' dread
To a weekends' drive:
With whom to sleep
And who may weep.

The motto of a single man
Dictates, "Get what you can,
In spite of a terrific stress:
Eat, drink, pay and undress!"

I have to leave this town
Before shit hits the fan;
I have to settle down
While I am still a man.

White Anchored Yachts

The light is fading.
The void of darkness
Like a concealed invading
Of something totally unknown,
That promised not to harm us;
Meantime, the dice was thrown.

A mirror doesn't reflect my face
As if I am not standing here,
As if my horse is in the race
To cease this short-lived year,
To catch my past and to return
Into my youth that chose to burn.
I badly want my glee to outlast
The darker time that never passed.

I slept. The vultures-memories
Descended on my chest;
I woke and pulled the draperies
To see the sunsets of the West;

Today, I finally discovered why
I love the seas. They never lie.

A few white anchored yachts
Are rocking their attractive hips;
Reminding of the seaport sluts
With whispering and luring lips.

My curiosity is utterly incurable,
Innocently intense and durable
With vastly unpredictable results;
Only the graveyards cure adults.

White Pearls, Black Ties

White pearls, black ties,
White ties, black pearls,
A spectacle for our eyes,
The pinnacle of our curse.

The grimaces are stronger
Than insincerity of smiles,
The shadows are no longer
Crossing our sunlit isles.

The highest entry fee
Into my church's steeple,
The glory of philanthropy
Resides in lesser people.

The wall of social divisions,
The oldest goddamned lesson,
Complies with new provisions
Designed by Smith & Wesson.

We estimate the studs,
We learn the pedigrees,
We praise bluebloods,
Infrequently the adoptees.

Dark portraits of forbearers,
The olden monies from afar,
Open the doors and barriers,
If you're married into money,
We'll remember who you are,
Yet, always call you honey.

A social prestige,
A tasty greasy dish,
A tasteless cloak,
Worn often as a yoke.

White pearls, black ties,
White ties, black pearls,
A spectacle for our eyes,
The pinnacle of our curse.

White Petals Whirl

I can no longer bear
My hiding in the woods,
I even dye my hair
To hide the silver roots.

Societies of laws
Hide friendships
Between the foes,
Societies of trends
Hide solitudes
Among the friends.

I wear my iron cuffs,
Their pins are rusted
As chuckles of a crow,
I left behind my bluffs,
My footsteps dusted
With the virgin snow.

Hey, doc, while I'm here,
Just cure my crazy mind
And I'll forever disappear,
The FBI won't ever find.

I am a lonesome boat,
Cut waters like a knife,
My memories still float
Over the river of my life.

White petals whirl
Like snow in July
As if a fallen girl
Sings me her lullaby,

My nightmares
Come and go,
My love affairs
Melt with that snow.

White Snow Falls

White snow falls
To cover our wilt,
To freeze decay,
The future rolls
Across that quilt
Above the fray.

Our last half-baked
Crusade
Collected forces of
Aggression,
To stop a useless
Masquerade
Of our unbearable
Obsession
With futile glorified
Success,
With our perpetual
Stress.

We watch the fearless
Stars,
Above lighthouses of
Hope,
But only a bloodthirsty
Mars
Leads us to the end of
Rope.

The train of memories
Is ready to arrive
Into the terminal of life,
A sparkly mirror
Of the flowing river

Rocks trembling image
Of a devastated village
Where brothers fought
And bled,
But memories don't
Wake the dead.

My well-dressed garden
Enjoys the Midas' touch,
A golden autumn gets a
Pardon
From gods who learned
Too much.

White Wings

I'm too lenient
With those who cheat,
I punish only those
Whom I reliably defeat.
I sin,
I win.

I hung a hammock
In the corner of my life,
It rocks and sways
It holds remains of futile,
Inessential things,
But only I remember
Where I have hidden
The precious treasures
Of my unending strife
For earthly pleasures,
During my happy days
When just a pair of wings
Kept me above the havoc.

White wings,
Black deeds,
My inner devil brings
Few ill-intentioned seeds.

My fortune blinks,
I'm a wreck,
I lost my wings,
But stacked the deck.

I just re-entered history
Before the rays of dawn,
I placed a bet,

I tried my best and won.
It was a thrilling victory,
Although a narrow one,
And yet,
The game still goes on.

Why

I dash across the sunlit snow,
A falcon cuts the sunlight flow,
Why do we always fight?
Why can't we let it go?
There's enough of light
Under the arches of rainbow.

Why do we try to break or bend?
Why can't we try to fix or mend?

Whether we are indicted or incited,
Both chairs reserved for the invited,
Both roads veer like the thrown dice
To gates of the abyss and paradise.

Don't wake me up,
Don't mess with my nightmares,
Don't spill illusions from my cup,
Let me ascend the promised stairs.

Wiggling Hips

Life is a half-lit motel lounge
Where men pick up the girls,
All they could scrounge
Without casting pricy pearls.
Whether a predator or prey,
Both crave to hit the hay.

My left-hand fingers
Pirouetting on the frets,
My right hand meanders
The tunes of red sunsets.
Beer from the door,
Free pretzels, a few tips.
I cannot take it anymore,
I hate these wiggling hips.
I play, I drink until I faint,
Then I become a saint.

The essence of integrity,
A promise kept.
In presence of a divine celebrity,
St. Thomas doubted then wept.
Only poor Mary recognized
Her teacher,
Who made her free, not richer,
Who saved her life from being
Stoned,
Who came to see her past
The crispification and beyond.

I'm neither jailed nor free,
I made the ploughshares
From bloody swords,
I walked the sea of Galilee,

Just mark my words.
I crossed the Rubicon
And burned the bridge,
I saw the promised paradise
And led you to its ridge,
Don't let them close your eyes.

Wines flow and hover
Like everlasting dawn,
I smell and swirl them
As an impatient lover,
I fall in love with them
As if I'm a lonely faun.

We never grow older
Around dining tables,
We only grow balder
In our soporific beds
As gluttony disables
Our stubborn heads.

I peeled the leather
Binding
Of a ragged ancient
Book,
The history is freed,
Here is the finding:
I had a clear-cut look,
Please, fill your glass,
I say, In Vino Veritas,
Drink wine and read.

The saints will render
Last steps of our lives,
So vulnerably tender,
So passionately wise.

Winner Takes All

Life makes the softest bed,
Though it's too hard to rest,
I try to earn my daily bread,
At times, I do my very best.

I watch a movie for my mind,
The film is "Seek and Hide",
A buddy of my joyous youth
Still running from the truth,
He hides from our oath,
Eternal loyalty from both,
The saints don't like his lies,
But they're busy in the skies.

He entertained his fright,
Meanwhile, I went to fight,
I heard the whistle,
The bullet missed,
My thick unshaven bristle
Went gray, war is a beast,
I could no longer walk,
I could no longer run,
I need no preacher's cloak,
I simply need a better gun.

I wipe my salty fear,
I lick my upper lip,
The enemy is near,
It's just a coin's flip
May start our strife,
Winner takes all,
Death wrestles life
To claim my soul.

Within the Lies

I danced away from questions,
I could have gotten lost
Between the old nostalgic photos
Of glories and atrocities of wars.
The sun has not yet set
On values versus pleasures
Of trusting in the Holy ghost
Who trails our church's whores.
I hold my breath but place a bet
On someone's useless trash
Against my ghostly treasures.

Old age is toying with my mind,
I can no longer find
My childhood friends,
Or movies with the happy ends.

Only a lifelong madness
Of the crooked mirrors
Reflects our everlasting sadness
And memories of fallen heroes;
The pain of those who knew
That our curiosity has gone,
That there is nothing new
Under the scorching sun.

Even the innocence of our souls
Drowned in quagmires of the past
Among the futile dreams and goals,
While our lives are quickly passed.

Being an actor is the only way of living
Within the lies as a fodder of existence,
Within a daily cover-up of our grieving;
Unfortunately, a noose
Becomes the path of least resistance.

Without Our Sins

I am a sobbing mess,
I am a snowless winter,
Scotch melts my stress
In an abandoned snifter.

The sun still beams
Above my hopes,
Then whips my dreams
And yanks the ropes.

It is the nature's farewell plot,
It is the winter's parting blow,
The miserable crunchy snow
Falls on the Lord's blind spot.

Two swirling brittle snowflakes,
The innocent and gentle twins
Without our horrible mistakes,
Without our inevitable sins,
Died in my trembling hands
As two inseparable friends.

I closed my weary eyes
To see a castle in the skies.

I'm floating downstream
Like an abandoned pup
Toward a stepping stone.
Don't interrupt my dream,
Don't try to wake me up,
Let me continue alone.

A fiery Elijah ride
Still lingering inside
Of every day I lived,
Of every blessing I received.

Without Peace in Sight

I looked far back
And knew full well,
I ran my moral track,
But wound up in hell.

I went across a hostile world,
Abandoned by the fighting horde,
A narrow path between two walls,
Amid the graveyards of the souls,
Without days, without nights,
Left by eternity of blinding lights.

No dusks, no dawns,
No stars, no bars,
Above the marching pawns,
Above the actors of the farce.

I begged, life opened doors
And I was shoved inside,
Into a carnival of wars
Without peace in sight.

I hope someone will live in peace,
A second mouse gets the cheese.

Without You

Widespread confusions,
My house door unlocked,
I am a victim of delusions,
Dazed and shell-shocked.

Dull hope or bright despair,
I am searching in the flare
In quest for evil or for good,
I wouldn't judge, God would.
I'm still basking in your glow,
I failed. Why did I let you go?

You blinded me with light
Of carnal knowledge,
I was naively horrified
By your desire to salvage
Ancient idols from the rust
And worship vanity 'n lust.

Life is a weary journey
From point A to point Z,
From early breakfast
Into a final "break 'n rest."

One monkey
Doesn't make a show,
Few chilly days
Don't bring the snow,
I crave a happy life,
Willing and ready,
I miss you, wife,
I need you, lady.

Come back, come back,
Whisper farewell to angels,
Without you, I walk a track
Surrounded by strangers.

A needle in a haystack,
You're invisible to saints,
I'll find, I'll bring you back,
Before my longing faints.

Worst Ever End

Best ever start,
Worst ever end,
Sunrise comes a la carte,
Sunset waits to descend.

Why do the neediest
End in a viper's nest?
Why do the greediest
Arrive to all the best?

Isn't it because that man
Was crucified
And memory has died?
Is it because the saints
Are old and far away?
Is it because
Our conscience faints,
Walking on feet of clay?

Haves and have-nots
Share hopes and wishes
As equals in this strife.
But if the days turn vicious,
The latter dwell
On filthy parking lots,
The haves reap fruits of life.

I'm an anarchist,
Lost in the midst
Of decent people.
I'm a subtle ripple,
I'm a surface dent.
I dwell on parking lots,
I can't afford the rent.

Worth More Alive

Larger-than-life,
Vague and opaque,
The gods of afterlife
Have got their cake.

I hear my brothers' mourning,
Over a boneyard every morning,
I hear their cries in silence
Of our camouflaged defiance.

I'm a brick-and-mortar guy
Along equations quid pro quo,
I didn't like those standers by
And swam against the flow.

I couldn't validate my wishes,
They turned into my dreams,
Life served me empty dishes,
Ignoring a discord of screams.

Am I worth more alive
Or dead,
Aside from where I'm today,
Must I divide my daily bread
Amid the fallen in the strive?
It's absolutely safe to say,
That I'm going home
To soothe my tortured soul,
That I'm going home
To break the dead-end wall.

I wanted to unfurl the knot,
But failed to pass the quiz,
I knew what God is not,
But didn't know what He is.

Worthy of Believing

In my pursuit of happiness
I wandered into emptiness
Of yet unknown science,
Wrapped in a loud silence.
As if I entered
The same old river twice,
As if I rendered
A set of loony rules
For a demented paradise
Inhabited by human mules.

I've heard as Judas cried:
"I've sinned. For I betrayed
Untarnished blood."
This too, "What's that to us?"
I trooped from west to east
In spite of rains and flood,
Then fell under the bus
To pick what Judas missed,
The diamonds in the mud.

I learned the art of giving,
The art of a redemptive love,
It was well-worthy of believing
In a fence-mending job thereof.

Not shrouded in the mystique,
I simply went a little deeper
Into inverted life, so to speak,
In which a loser is a keeper.

Under a glittery giftwrap
Of an unbearable control,
It's a conniving mousetrap
Imprisoning my anxious soul.
A "horse-and-buggy" traveler
No more,
I haven't shut the secret door.

Wreck

What do we know
About our fading goals?
What do we know
About our soaring souls?

Our globe submerging
Into the swampy tide
Up to its equator-neck,
Life's desperately urging
To find a visionary angel-guide
To lead us out of this total wreck.

We wear our tragic masks
That tightly camouflage
Our imperious pedigree;
We still pursue the tired tasks
Of reaching majesty or a mirage
Of our ancestral glee,
Of seeing a multilayered blue
Of the eternal Mediterranean Sea.

The splendid depth our fathers knew.

Yet My Desires Prevailed

My sailboat is dancing
On the trembling ripples
Ran by a morning breeze;
My pleasure doubles, triples,
Our Mother Nature cannot sing,
But eagerly performing a striptease.

Her hips were beaming youth,
Her lips were hiding truth,
Yet my desires prevailed,
I morphed into a conman bailed.

I jumped off a steep cliff of glee
Into the precipice of yet unknown love,
Reminding me of everlasting salty sea,
Quite rarely tender, often rough.

I sail through icy darkness
Of my challenging existence,
Across a blinding starkness
Of my inherited persistence.

My greed began to overweigh
My skills and my desire to thrive,
Beyond the final inning of a play
Or the first inning of a strife.

We are forever roped together
With fruitless axioms of science,
With the annoying birds of feather,
And with the consequence of silence.

The times stood still,
I missed; the others made a kill;
I was still working on the paradigm,
The others were revolving on a dime.

You Are a Hand; I Am a Glove

You are a mystery, a riddle,
You are not a country fiddle,
You are the greatest violin,
The prize no one can win.

I can't reverse the river's flow,
I can't adore sunshine at night,
I can't prevent the wintry snow,
But I can see the godsent light.

It is the color of your eyes
Descending to a quiet river,
It is the everlasting skies
Ascending from its mirror.

You are a goddess of perfection
Belonging to the world above,
You are a sign of resurrection
Of a nostalgic ecstasy of love.

Love of a gorgeous woman
Is like a gentle fresh bouquet,
I hold it while it's blooming,
Tomorrow, it may fade away.

I am doing time in jail,
I am a prisoner of love,
I am a lifer with no bail,
You are a hand; I am a glove.

You Are my Christmas Gift

The clouds slowly drift
Like angels in the blue,
You are my Christmas gift,
I am ready to unwrap you.

I'll eat you with the spoon,
I'll be making love to you,
After the snooping moon
We'll roll in morning dew.

We'll try to brush aside
My critics-nasty vipers;
They get in the way a lot,
And leave behind a mess.
I guess, their moms forgot
To change their diapers
And wipe their callousness.

Above the poets' heads
The sword of Damocles
Demands a frank striptease.
We slyly pull the threads
And gentle morning breeze
Caresses our verses,
Our forever naked trees.

Enjoy the tongues of fire,
Peel off your nylon lashes,
The fireside of my desire
Will scorch us into ashes.

I love the Christmas time,
It is my joy; it is my rhyme.

You Are My Spring

I spin the globe,
I dream of France,
I pull my lucky lobe,
I fall into a trance.

I see a headless silhouette
Silently walks into my room,
Forever young Marie-Antoinette
I am your proud fearless groom.

You are brighter than bonfire,
You are the star of my desire,
You are my dream and fate,
You are my gorgeous date.

You lost your head,
A penny to the dust,
Let's break the bread,
I want to win your trust.

Finish your bread,
Finish your drink,
Come to my bed,
You are my spring.

You Never Go Away

Make love and hush,
Enjoy the crazy night,
Even the roses blush,
When ready for a fight.

You never go away,
I never missed you,
I've never been alone,
My world is always gray,
But I'm red, white and blue,
I can't become your clone.

Your lovely witty thoughts
Have earned my admiration,
I sent few thank you notes,
And left this gloomy station.

I'm a walking dead,
The bloody footprints
Of our broken hearts
Lead us into a mire,
My trembling hands
Can't strike the flints,
Can't throw the darts,
Can't launch the fire.

These days, I write
Without words,
These days, I fight
Without swords.

I drag my load,
I climb the walls,
I touch the skies,
I cross the road
Below our souls
To kiss your eyes.

You Played Me Like a Violin

You played me like a violin,
You barely moved your fingers,
I coped with pain of my chagrin,
Only the pain of love still lingers.

I watched my sorrow's flight,
I heard the elegies of love,
I wrote this requiem at night
As cries of a wounded dove.

I raked a few fading stars
For your sendoff bouquet,
You were an actress in this farce,
You left me with the winds of May.

The ice of your abrupt farewell
Will never soothe my wounds,
I'll survive this freezing trail,
I'll embrace the sunny dunes.

The moon above the gable
Looks like a midnight chime,
My boat, a sentimental cradle
Rocks on the waves of time.
In harbors for the noiseless,
I navigate amid the voiceless.

I'm living below the spell
Of ancient hills of hopes,
The ice of your farewell
Still sliding by their slopes.

You Put Away My Fire

You are my guiding star,
When you don't lead, I fail,
Please rush, fly from afar,
Light up my shaded trail.

You put away my fire
With waterfalls of love,
You are an icon of desire,
An angel from above.

You come into my day,
I kiss your honey lips,
You are a flower of May,
I only hope nobody rips.

You see my tears of joy,
I reached my goal;
Tomorrows won't destroy
A haven for my soul.

My verses miss their virtues,
I am lost among the troubles,
I cannot bear life's tortures,
My body violently wobbles,
And finally, I understood,
I am preaching to the choir,
My revelation is too crude,
It's hard to call myself a liar.

You Said

You said,
Don't ever let me go,
Don't,
I'll cry and cry until
I won't.

Life is
A savior or a sinner,
Life is
A loser or a winner,
A gourmet meal or
Just a TV dinner.

Life is
A mischievous charm
Of a self-effacing thief,
Life is
A swirling golden leaf,
Hopelessly descending
With an enticing charm,
Life is
The end of rainy days,
Life is
A fiery sunset's blaze,
When flakes of snow
Must die like actors
Of a dramatic show,
Life is
A sweet romantic craze.

Life was
A merciless, cruel winter,
Surely not the promised
Paradise,
Life was
A long-distance runner,
Not a sprinter,
My heart morphed into
Solid ice.

I died, I closed my eyes,
I didn't hear your cries.

You Tried to Hide

I'll become the sun
To wrap you in my light,
I'll become the moon
To let you sleep at night,
I'll become a wind
To whisper in your ears
That love has gone
With laughs and cheers.

You hid from all
Your empty soul,
You always lied,
You tried to hide
Two frozen eyes,
Two cubes of ice.

You were a needle
In a large haystack,
I solved that riddle,
Love is a cul de sac.

I picked few puzzles
to defuse
The seven godsent
hues,
The seven rainbow's
sins,
The seven primal days
Of our genes.

I met no angels-saviors
Amid "Don't kill and love
Your vicious neighbors,"
I am a merciless raven,
Not a softhearted dove,
Deserving a safe haven.

You Win the Battles...

The night is young,
The bubbly wrapped in ice,
L'amour est morte,
It is not yet the news,
This song is still unsung,
I'll sing it for a price,
And yet, life is too short
To waste it on the blues.

Why do you need to know
The truth, that only seems,
Where all my sorrows flow
To hide the pain of dreams?

Why do you need to know
When angels play in marching bands
And nightly stars of poor Van Gogh
Fall into his brother's caring hands?

Why do you want to know
That I don't love you anymore?
You reap exactly what you sow,
You win the battles, lose the war.

It is so hard to find a friend,
It is much easier to fall in love,
It is so easy to ascend,
It is so hard to fall into a bluff.

L'amour est morte,
It is not quite the news,
But life is so damn short
To waste it on the blues.

Young Lieutenant

He never left that battlefield,
This man will never grow old,
A friend of mine was killed,
I touched his neck. Too cold.

I tore a bent dog tag
Off the young lieutenant,
The others laid a flag
Over this uninvited tenant.

His heart fell on the field,
His gentle spirit soared,
His destiny was sealed,
He went to see his Lord.

I saw a quiet dignity
In that impatient man,
As if he craved infinity,
But didn't walk, he ran.

The heart of gold,
The nerves of steel,
Another trail is cold,
Another Navy Seal.
Another photo on my wall,
Another tragic curtain call.

Young Lilacs' Twigs

The moon is glowing,
It knows our intrigues,
The wind is blowing.
Young lilacs' twigs
Whip dusty windows
Of my country digs.

I learned to bear my pain,
Friends say, it's all in vain,
And yet, my eyes are dry,
I never learned to cry.

I am revisiting my past,
My wars with wives and lovers,
I am a sinking boat; no mast,
Only my albatross still hovers.

Someone may take,
Someone may give,
I would prefer to lie and fake
Than to forget or to forgive.

I choked my wicked youth
In favor of aesthetics,
I feverously try to soothe
The scars of my genetics.

Acknowledgments

I am deeply and endlessly grateful to Judith Broadbent for her skilled professional guldens and generous stewardship; for her unyielding yet wise editing which gave me enough room to exercise my whims.

To Anna Dikalova for her kind ideas and a firm belief In my success.

To a great artist, Mary Anne Capeci, who allowed me to use her painting for the cover of this book.

To all my friends for their continuous and gently Expressed motivations.

Thanks, y'all.

Printed in the United States
by Baker & Taylor Publisher Services